Dear Matthew,

I will always appreciate the gift you gave me allowing me to speak to your spiritual community.

Your grace and openness that stayed alive all this time.

You are a blessing!

Love and Peace

Maureen

YOUR ESSENTIAL WHISPER

Six Distinct Ways to Recognize, Trust, and Follow Inner Guidance with Absolute Certainty

Vanessa Tabor Wesley
and La Rue Eppler

iUniverse, Inc.
New York   Bloomington

Your Essential Whisper

Six Distinct Ways to Recognize, Trust, and Follow Inner Guidance with Absolute Certainty

iUniverse books may be ordered through booksellers or by contacting:

iUniverse
1663 Liberty Drive
Bloomington, IN 47403
www.iuniverse.com
1-800-Authors (1-800-288-4677)

Because of the dynamic nature of the Internet, any Web addresses or links contained in this book may have changed since publication and may no longer be valid. The views expressed in this work are solely those of the author and do not necessarily reflect the views of the publisher, and the publisher hereby disclaims any responsibility for them.

ISBN: 978-0-595-45422-8 (pbk)
ISBN: 978-0-595-50859-4 (cloth)
ISBN: 978-0-595-89735-3 (ebk)

iUniverse Rev Date 11/14/2008
Printed in the United States of America

Contents

Acknowledgments.. vii

Introduction xv

The Prologue...1

    I Am with You Always – Experiencing the Soul 3

Section One Recognizing Your Essential Whisper...........................13

    1   God by Any Other Name – Your Essential Whisper................15

    2   Snapshot-Click – The Bookmarks in Your Life 21

    3   Collapsed Time and Space – The Eternal...............................27

    4   Urge – The Energy that Guides Your Next Step......................33

    5   Wonderment – The Presence of Awe.....................................39

    6   Knowing – The Message of Resonance 49

    7   Inspiration – The Energy of Creation 57

Section Two – Trusting Your Essential Whisper 63

    8   A Template for Trust – Creating the Experience of Trust.........65

    9   The One Action to Take – Five Simple Acknowledgements 71

10 The One Decision to Make - Four Channels to Awareness 77

11 The Beliefs that Block Trust – Uncovering the Symptoms of
Resistance...83

12 Your Intrinsic Design – There's a Blueprint in You 99

13 Attract Your Heartfelt Desires with Certainty – Allow the
Whisper to Do the Work...111

Section Three – Following Your Essential Whisper........................ 121

14 Interactions with Your Essential Whisper – Receiving Distinct
Messages 123

15 Guidance vs. Disguise – Maneuvering Through the Noise of
Thought...143

16 Your Essential Nature –Embracing Inner Joy 155

Section Four – Creating a Partnership with Your Whisper 161

An Eight-Week Practice Guide and Journal 163

Epilogue – The End of the Story...189

Appendix A – The Anchoring Meditation 193

Appendix B – Resistance and Values Procedure................................. 197

Appendix C - About Evo-K... 201

Chapter Notes and Resources.. 203

ACKNOWLEDGMENTS

By La Rue Eppler

My life and work have been touched by so many people over the last nineteen years. In my attempt to acknowledge everyone, I feel certain that there will be someone I have overlooked. For those, please accept my apology; I invite you into your heart to feel my sincere gratitude, which awaits you there.

Without the conscious awareness of my Essential Whisper, this book would not exist. Although the Whisper has been with me my entire life, for the last fifteen years it has been my daily companion, navigating my steps like lanterns softly lighting my way, and for that I am forever grateful.

My life turned in a new direction in 1993 when Dr. John F. Demartini introduced me to the voice of my soul. To this day, I still ask my soul the most simple question, which elicits profound guidance: What do you want me to know? Without fail, it responds in the perfect moment in time.

In 1994, a remarkable woman, Byron Katie, walked through the doors of my life. Her process, The Work, taught me to question the beliefs that held me prisoner in my own mind. The days she spent in my home, as I observed how she lives in sublime harmony with *what is*, gave me a glimpse of a new way of being. The first time I was consciously aware of loving myself, I was in her presence. I'm grateful.

My endless thanks go to my cherished friend, Dr. Fabrizio Mancini, who inspires greatness simply with his presence. With his encouragement, I began to stretch the walls of my comfort zone when he nudged me to hone my speaking skills at a local coffee shop every Wednesday evening in 1997. Who would have ever guessed that those coffee talks for twenty to thirty people would ultimately lead to an international audience?

Eighteen years ago, I personally vowed that if I ever wrote a book, I would acknowledge Roz Burnham. Roz followed her Essential Whisper one Tuesday afternoon, when after having her first session with me, she suggested exchanging office space in return for sessions with me while my business became established. She so generously mentored me in the law of attraction long before it was ever called that.

And to my clients; without them, this work would never have had the opportunity to evolve into excellence. I thank each and every one of them. A special thanks to Marilyn Ridings, one of my original clients, for her undying belief in me and for offering her brilliant insights and loving suggestions over the years. Blessings to Debbie Berndt, who suggested, after she made a long-distance move and was no longer able to do face-to-face sessions, that I facilitate phone sessions for her. Overnight, my service became global when I discovered that I could use Applied Kinesiology on myself to access the wisdom of her soul, despite her location. Suddenly, I knew that I could assist someone on the other side of the world as easily as if they were sitting in my office, looking into my eyes.

To my students who were so passionate about the results they received from Evolutional Kinesiology that they became facilitators. There are numerous facilitators in the United States and England, and since I do not want to overlook anyone, I will leave them unnamed, although they remain deeply, deeply embedded in my heart. I am grateful for each of them and the future ones to come. Special thanks go to Lia Marie Danks and Mary Helen Kuehner for their tireless editing of the ebook version of *Your Essential Whisper*. I am deeply grateful to Erika Nelson who gives endlessly with pure motive, always thinking about how she can open a door of opportunity or provide professional feedback to improve our materials and courses.

Tina Azamar, my technology angel, who taught me about the importance of a web presence. I am blessed to have been under her tutelage and care as she patiently taught me about twenty-first-century business. And now there is Carol Cody, my friend, student, and current technical partner, who holds a big vision for our many projects.

To the many extraordinary people who offered the testimonials found sprinkled throughout this book. They have lived this work and been as much a source of inspiration and strength for me as my work and life have been to them. My love goes to all of you.

My endless gratitude goes to Dharma Gaines and Emily and Roger Terry who each followed their Essential Whisper and, in doing so, opened the doors of opportunity in England and Europe. I'm blessed by their friendship and for the beautiful people I continue to meet and serve because they each walked into my life.

To my precious friend, the late Dr. Edmund Tyska, who took me under his wing and believed in me long before I even had a clue who I was. My life is still touched by the ripple effect his life had on mine. His encouragement to embrace my spirit and to follow the path of my heart changed the direction of my life forever.

And to the Hasty and Jones family, who walked through the doors as clients but walked out as family. I love them all: Kim, Billy, Virginia, Kenny, Pam, Logan, and Kali Brie.

What would life be without the beautiful souls sent into our lives called friends? I am blessed to have many authentic friends who each have made a beautiful impact upon my life and my work, each in their own unique way: Teddie Bussey, Mary Stillwell, Keta Dodson, Elizabeth Brooks, Bea Lovejoy, Tony Cecala, and Felicia Weiss.

And to my girlfriends, Nancy Grace, Rita Reneaux, and Bobbi Stein, who continue to love and support me despite my absence from the group while I dedicated full attention to this book, my travels, and my work, always welcoming me with open arms upon my return. I offer a most heartfelt thanks to Wendy Darling for coaching me in the development of one of my first talks many years ago, but most important, for teaching me about true friendships and taking my hand, walking me through some very rough times in my life, and loving me all the way.

To Lynne Russell who, so appreciative of what our work has done for her, invested two years, thousands of dollars, and endless love making a documentary about her intuitive journey, as a tribute to us. We are honored!

And to Audrey Chapman, who was so captivated by *Your Essential Whisper* that she couldn't put it down due to the many connections she was making with her Essential Whisper. As she shared her epiphanies with me, I felt joy and relief to know that this book was accomplishing its mission—to assist *you* in realizing your connection to *your* Essential Whisper, making this book a story about your life, not mine.

And of course, to my precious friend and colleague, Vanessa Wesley, for following her inner Urge to call me out of the blue to offer to write this book. Because of her, this book became much more than I could have ever written by myself, and it morphed from my book to our book. She deserves a crown fit for a queen for transcribing hundreds of pages of interviews and conversations with me, turning those transcripts into a readable book and loving the process every step of the way.

Super huge thanks goes to Tim and Melissa Capper, who have long believed in me, and to Tim for the video he lovingly shot and put his magic touch to for *Your Essential Whisper*, our multimedia ebook.

Enormous thanks goes to Lila Lear for being my first teacher in applied kinesiology and helping me cut through confusion to reach my true self for the first time. My gratitude also goes to Daniel Whiteside and Gordon Stokes for their brilliance and development of One Brain, a remarkable methodology for rewiring your brain and making it come alive!

Enormous, endless love and gratitude go to my precious mother and father for giving me life. Dad taught me that if something bad happens, it's because God is trying to give you something even better. Mother taught me inner strength, both by her words and her living example. This list of acknowledgements would be incomplete without acknowledging my beloved one and only sister, Barbara, who has been a friend, sister, and mother figure to me. And to her husband and my brother-in-law, Ken, who has been there for me in dire times of need. They took me into their home while I healed from divorce.

Finally, I am forever grateful to my extraordinary son Ben who, from early childhood, danced to the beat of his own drum, and by doing so, was the catalyst that jolted me from the trance of indoctrination. Without him, I don't know where my life would have taken me. This I know for sure: I'm blessed to have the gift of him, his raw honesty, his humor, and his radiant, embracing love in my life—the kind of love that calls me every year on Mother's Day *and* Father's Day to offer his gratitude, always reminding me of how grateful he is to me for being a mother and father to him.

And to you, I send love for acting on the Urge you felt to read this book. You will be blessed in unimaginable ways by recognizing, trusting, and following your inner Whisper as it lovingly navigates your journey through life.

Acknowledgments

By Vanessa Tabor Wesley

When one is over fifty and writes her first book, the list of acknowledgments could get rather long.

So far, I've lived an extremely happy life, and everyone who touched it, over the years or even for a day or a moment, in some way, some Whisper of a way, had a significant part in the unfolding of this book and the joy I've experienced during these five decades. Yet I am going to keep this brief, although I implore all of my dear friends and clients across the globe to know that in my heart is a burgeoning, unstoppable love for you, whether or not your name is listed.

There are a few people, however, who cannot go unnamed. My dear departed mother, Katherine, whose worn sofa I sat on for two days while I had my first dialogue with a higher voice. She always encouraged me, setting me on my path of health and wellness. She quietly built a self-esteem in me that enabled me to always have connection to inner wisdom. She taught me to trust myself. Amazingly, she has taught me as many lessons from beyond as she ever did in life, as I continue to remember her voice and wise words when most needed.

A mother is not only biological; she can sweep into your life and give it a richness and depth that belies blood connection. Lillian married my dad over twenty years ago and has been Mom ever since. The day I told her that I wanted to attend a month-long training with La Rue but didn't know how I could with a four-year-old, she, without hesitation, said, "You *must* do this," and jumped on the next plane. I am eternally grateful for her staunch support and faith that I would eventually get this message out.

My dad, John Tabor, taught me how much a father can love a daughter. He called me "the psychiatrist" in my teens, said he was sure I would fix everyone, and then stayed on the sidelines, encouraging each of my changes, ideas, endeavors, and comings and goings. He's my quiet cheerleader. Thank you, Dad. Babalooski!

If you're fortunate, you've got one or two really good girlfriends. I've got dozens, but no truer friend than the one I have in Gina Wesley. Our friendship began at nine when we climbed apple trees and bellowed songs by the Supremes. At twenty-four, I married her brother, and at fifty, she told me, "Vanessa, no one will see your dream but you, if you don't live it now, then when?" She stuck by me for over forty years as I ranted and raved about hearing inner guidance, and she managed to only once call me fanatical. My gratitude for her trust, humor, and loving friendship, as well as her own deep spiritual wisdom, cannot be contained in words.

In 2002, I stopped seeing clients and doing sessions and decided to home-school my daughter. Two home-schooling moms insisted I come out of the closet and offer this work again. Nancy Rossi and Judy Davis saw in me and in this work something I had put aside. They lovingly pulled it back out of me and have been by my side, championing this whole process. If it weren't for them, this book would not be in your hands. Thank you for your friendship; I am blessed.

To my "hanging out" girls, Sandra Woods, Joanie Bryant, Anne Johnson, and Pam Rodgers, who have told me over and over while we sipped apple martinis, "Go for it!" (And, yes, you can hear inner guidance and have an occasional 'tini.) To Brenda Carridine, who stood across my kitchen counter back in 1999 and said, "Vanessa, you've got to tell people about this." Your words and that Snapshot have stayed deeply in my heart.

To all the devoted teachers, authors, and guides I have had the great blessing to know through the hundreds of books I've read. Some I've met— Byron Katie, for one, whose simple inquiry has helped me find incredible peace. Then, of course, there's La Rue, who touched my life in unfathomable ways. Her warm spirit and gentle manner are only surpassed by her keen vision to see this work touch countless lives. I am blessed beyond measure to have her as a friend and business colleague.

The teacher who has had the greatest impact on me, opening the door to my soul, is my darling daughter, Taylor Alexis. At five years old, she said that she came here to give love to everyone. I felt that love the moment she was conceived. She is my biggest enthusiast, although often, she had to e-mail me to get my attention. Thank you for missing quite a few home-cooked meals and tolerating my distractions. Your bubbling joy, laughter, music, hugs, and kisses have helped me burn many a midnight candle.

And finally, to my dearest husband, Sterling, whose name, meaning "of the finest quality," is befitting. It's been thirty years since those fateful two days listening to a higher voice on my mother's sofa as I questioned leaving Boston and my modeling career to join him in Louisiana. Forty-eight hours later, at the end of the dialogue, when higher voice asked, "So, would you rather be with him or without him?" I knew my answer and took a Greyhound bus to Louisiana. Snapshots abound to tell me our souls are entwined. Thank you for all you've done to help get this message out of me and onto these pages, everything from teaching me PowerPoint to making sure I had a decent computer. And, most of all, thank you, thank you, thank you for your love, generosity, and kindness.

Introduction

Is every person connected to an innate and divine wisdom? If so, can anyone access that connection? Sacred literature from all the major religions declares that we do have that ability. Yet, if that is true, really true, then there must be a way to explain it so that anyone, anywhere, would know exactly how to feel and know that connection. Further, if it's true that anyone, anywhere, has access to a divine wisdom, why are so many lives in turmoil? Why is it so hard for the average person to recognize this wisdom—what many refer to as God? Have you ever wondered about that? We have. Answering those questions became the intention of this book. The challenge was, is there an easy way to know—and to know with certainty—how to listen to inner guidance, no matter who you are, what religion you practice, or which culture you come from? That's a pretty big challenge; wouldn't you agree?

We wondered if we were up to the mission. But then, an interesting phenomenon occurred. The book seemed to write itself. In the most delicious and awesome way, we'd find the exact words to use and the exact meaning to convey. We became very good friends with the dictionary and thesaurus, searching for specific, clear-cut ways to describe the experiences of connecting to inner guidance. No fluff. No misunderstanding. Eventually, an easier language explaining inner access to divine wisdom was born.

But that's not how the book began.

So, let's go back to the beginning. Originally, we intended to tell a story. It was to be the story of the extraordinary unfolding of LaRue's life and how she came to birth a revolutionary process. In 1989, LaRue was trained in a form of applied kinesiology. It was an intense training, which covered specific processes for releasing and neutralizing emotional stress. There were a variety of specific modalities, processes, and sequential steps involved when working with clients. The methodology was insightful, and her training changed her life in deep and profound ways.

A couple of years later, she discovered that the process she was using with clients had morphed into its own unique system. Her clients were experiencing intense and life-changing results, and her practice was expanding. People were clamoring to be trained in what she was doing. Quite unaware that she had developed anything particularly different than what she was taught, she would send people requesting training to her original teachers. Yet each person would return and exclaim, "That's not what you do!"

Eventually, LaRue realized that she had organically tapped into an aspect of kinesiology not being taught anywhere else. She had discovered something amazing. By simply asking questions during the session, such as "What do we do next?" she would be directed to the next step in the session. The client's unconscious wisdom would take over. Individual sessions were being customized from the innate intelligence of the client! She never had to guess or use a series of predetermined techniques or steps. This was mind-blowing and was the beginning of the work now known as Evolutional Kinesiology (Evo-K).[1] Her training evolved, transforming itself from mere technique into a process embodying a spiritual and evolutionary component.

After repeated requests from friends and clients, LaRue decided to teach what she knew and held her first formal facilitator training in 1997. That's when we met. I was trained in that first class. Since then, Evo-K facilitators have sprung up in the United States and the United Kingdom.

~~~~~~~~~~~~~~~~~~~~~~~~~~~~~~~~~~

Ten years later, in 2007, we came together to write a book about Evo-K. We both felt an urge (hint: this is one of the six distinct connections to inner guidance) to write a book. We wanted to expose the extraordinary unfolding of LaRue's life, document the blossoming of this work, and outline an easy and basic form of muscle testing for personal well-being. We compiled over four hundred pages of transcripts. It was an amazing process, albeit tedious. We bubbled with excitement, visualizing people all over the globe using this personal process to effectively experience peace. We knew from our clients that by the end of an Evo-K session, they've experienced peace. And whether they hold onto it or not, once peace is felt—even briefly, even for an instant—that moment transforms them. Peace is our nature, and once we remember it, once we taste it, we can always return to the experience of it. Peace doesn't leave us; peace is who we are. We couldn't wait to tell the world!

Yet something, some subtle and elusive piece of the puzzle, was missing. We'd sit curled up on the sofa, telling our stories and sharing experiences.

Squeals of excitement would peal forth as we found our lives had been on parallel paths. However, we wondered if others would feel confident getting kinesiology in a book. Would they know by reading a book how to do this process with certainty? Or would they question the validity of their own responses?

Evolutional Kinesiology uses the body as a biofeedback mechanism through muscle response feedback.[2] This gentle process of muscle testing allows the facilitator to receive movement from the client's two outstretched arms, which indicate "yes or true" or "no or not true." The muscles themselves aren't being tested. The muscles (or arms) respond to specific questions and act as a biofeedback system—through a strong hold or gentle release—giving yes or no answers.

This specialized form of physiological response identifies specific stressors in the body. In private Evo-K sessions, clients are guided to the emotional causes of these stressors and are led to their very own cellular intelligence, which contains all the memories, experiences, and perceptions of the individual. People have experienced profound truths and wisdom in Evo-K sessions. They'd feel refreshed and renewed. The stress they came into the session with was effectively neutralized and dissolved. But sometimes, not having complete confidence and assuredness when on their own, they'd go home after a session and have doubt or reassert habitual patterns, because they simply didn't know how to recognize and trust their own guidance. Eventually, we discovered the subtle and elusive missing piece of the puzzle. There was a question that begged to be answered—the question that has been asked by countless people throughout the ages:

"How do we really know when we are hearing from inner guidance and not the voices in our head?"

And that was the problem of putting kinesiology in a book. We knew and trusted our respective experiences of recognizing inner guidance, but it wasn't easy to clearly describe it to someone else. One has to have the experience of something to believe that it's real to him. You see, what we found missing, the missing puzzle piece, was an everyday language that helped people to know—with certainty—how to recognize, trust, and follow their essential and intrinsic wisdom. Telling others our experiences wasn't enough. We'd have to answer that question.

LaRue met what introduced itself to her as her *soul* one fateful day in a workshop, and from that point on, developed a partnership. She had a close relationship to intuitive guidance. In 1978, at twenty-three, I experienced a two-day dialogue with what introduced itself to me as my *higher voice*, and which has never left. The names we had for these experiences were different, but the sensations we felt were exactly the same. During our conversations, we uncovered the specific sensations that connect us to inner guidance and the distinct experiences that give rise to those sensations. That's when the *Six Distinct Experiences* was born.

Each of these six experiences has discernable sensations that you feel in your body, deep within your being. This internal guidance, with its distinguishable sensations, is what we call your Essential Whisper. It is essential, intrinsic, and always there for you.

That's when the direction of this book changed.

No longer would this be a practical guide, teaching you kinesiology. Filled with inspiration, we wanted you to know how you've already been *spoken* to, how you've already connected to your Whisper, and how you can access this for yourself without any technology, methodology, or system. Consider this: when someone you know very well calls you on the phone and says, "Hi, it's me!" do you recognize his voice? Sure you do! Voices have very distinct patterns called voice prints, and they are unique just like fingerprints. It's the same with your Essential Whisper. The sensations of this innate guidance have a distinct print, and they feel a certain way to you. You will come to recognize the Whisper's voice signature just the way you recognize the voice of your beloved.

Your Essential Whisper connects you to your divine nature and your inner guidance, and shows you how to do so with *absolute certainty*, anytime, no matter where you are, without any special techniques or methods.

Absolute certainty—that's a pretty bold statement, isn't it? Yet people from all walks of life are thirsting for this connection! Have you taken a look at the bookstore shelves in the self-help and spirituality sections lately? People want certainty in their lives. People are looking for ways to just have some peace as they handle their daily routines, raise kids, and go to work. People want to know how to make the best decisions; people want to make the *right* decisions. They want to know how to live with deep meaning, with a sense of purpose and fulfillment. People want to have financial independence. They want time to romp on the floor with the kids, go shopping with no worries, do work they love, see the world, and experience life fully and passionately.

So how can we make the bold assertion that you will know these sensations and distinct experiences with absolute certainty? We can because ...

We did something extraordinary.

We verified the information using kinesiology! We used the very methodology used with clients over the past nineteen years to validate and substantiate the information in this book! Kinesiology is a physiological biofeedback system that operates similar to a lie detector. When something being tested is true or affirming, the muscle being used to verify the information will hold strong. When something being tested is not true, then the muscle will go weak. Kinesiology applied correctly tells the truth.[3]

Do you find this hard to believe? This is not new information, although it may be the first time you've encountered it. Applied kinesiology has been around for several decades and has been scientifically studied and used by doctors and practitioners in many fields for quite some time. LaRue has been using her unique method for over nineteen years; and as a facilitator and practitioner in my private practice, I have used this process she taught me for over eleven years. Kinesiology offers the definitive way to bypass what we believe to be true and instead locate what is actually true

Do you remember the question that started this introduction? "Does every person have the ability to intentionally connect to innate divine wisdom?" When tested using kinesiology, the answer is yes.

What if everyone got this? What if everyone understood the very basic and easy ways to know with certainty how to recognize inner guidance? How much easier would it be for you, for example, to make decisions following the essential part of you that knows the truth? Wouldn't that be fabulous? The doctrine "God directs our steps" would become real and true for you.

Imagine if you could know exactly what those steps are, recognize the Whisper's guidance, and trust and follow its direction with certainty. Imagine if your life was lived with deep, abiding peace and pleasure.

The best part is, you've already done this. You've already experienced these sensations. You've already experienced the six occurrences of these sensations all throughout your life. So how would your life change if you did this intentionally, with increasing consistency?

We want you to have the direct experience of talking to God. Have you ever wondered how to have a dialogue, a conversation, with God? We tell you exactly how to do that in Chapter 14, Interactions with Your Essential Whisper.

Please understand, this is not a religious book; it has no rules or dogma. It is a book that shows you how to connect to an inner wisdom that speaks to you through the sensations of your body. Once you recognize these distinct feelings, you'll make decisions easily and effortlessly. You'll stop fighting yourself, you'll stop sabotaging your dreams, and you'll stop second-guessing your decisions.

Throughout the book, we've retained the essence of a living room chat. We've refrained from using outside references, scientific language, and documentation. We've kept the language clear and easy, defining concepts along the way. We tell you stories from our experiences and from our hearts. We did not include many quotes from well-known philosophers and poets or from religious and sacred texts. Instead, some of the most profound wisdom we've ever heard has come from everyday people. Connected to inner wisdom, each of us is an inspired poet when we speak from this place.

Don't you love stories? Most people do. Many of us relate to stories; we connect to the underlying archetype of a story, its implicit and inherent message. When stories touch our lives and hearts, it is often because we recognize a part of ourselves in their unfolding drama. There are lots of stories in *Your Essential Whisper*, vignettes of connecting points from LaRue's life and a few thrown in from mine, as well. We've also included several stories shared with us by people who have had direct experiences connecting to inner guidance.

Stories are personal connecting points, and their purpose is to help each of us locate the messages of love and remind us of our divine nature. This is their only purpose. For a moment, think about the story of your own life. Notice how events flow from one to the other, as if by design. Notice what stands out for you, what pops into your memory. These are your significant connecting points, and that is what is meant by "stories are personal connecting points."

The sensations, feelings, and emotions within stories speak deeply to us; the feelings conveyed by the storyteller connect us. Have you noticed how, when you're listening to someone tell you a personal story, that even if you can't relate to the event or situation, you can relate to the feelings being communicated? This is our wonderful commonality. This is how we are connected and united.

Our stories will help you find connecting threads in your story and how you too are led to the perfect unfolding in your life. They are doorways that will open your own recognition of these significant occurrences in your life. However, it isn't until you intentionally and consciously acknowledge these connections as guidance in your life that you will sit in complete confidence that you too can access this wisdom for yourself.

In Chapter 9, we give you five simple ways to acknowledge inner guidance and receive your messages. It isn't enough, however, to know the sensations of inner guidance; you have to know what it feels like when you ignore or resist your Essential Whisper. Have you ever told yourself, "I knew I should have done that?" You had a clear hit on the direction to take or decision to make, but you didn't follow it, and later you regretted it. We clearly define resistance, its symptoms, and even the specific thoughts you are bound to have.

We don't make you guess. There's a big chart (Chapter 15) that specifically compares the voice of wisdom to the voice (thoughts) in your head. You will know how to uncover the deceptive qualities of resistance that influence you to ignore your Essential Whisper. Most important, you will learn how to free yourself from the limiting beliefs and fears that keep most people from listening to and following inner guidance.

You will discover you are perfectly designed with a unique *intrinsic blueprint* with your own set of inherently established values. You will understand the difference between your intrinsic values and the values of your *belief system*. When these two sets of values are not aligned, it is difficult to attract what your heart desires. Whenever we try to go after what we think we should do or have, we step outside of living authentically and intrinsically.

Life unfolds without struggle when you live from your individualized intrinsic print and not by someone else's set of values. You will easily do things that naturally align with your nature, talents, and gifts. You will no longer need to defend or justify to yourself or to others why you love what you do or why you are pursuing your unique vision and dream. No one can express your vision the way you do. *Your Essential Whisper* will guide you every step of the way, and you will enjoy true happiness.

We want you to know, without any doubt, that inner guidance exists. The possibility for this intimate relationship with your essential nature exists, and we all have the ability to experience this inner connection. We've given you a language—a set of guideposts—for you to awaken yourself to your soul, to your higher voice. Our intention for you is that you find it harder to ignore your own sweet internal wisdom than you would to follow its guidance. Our hope for you is that you find following your essential guidance to be the easiest thing to do.

Vanessa Tabor Wesley, 2008

THE PROLOGUE

By La Rue

I Am Always Here For You

Experiencing the Soul

In my late twenties, I discovered I really wanted my name to be Freedom La Rue. As a little girl in church, anytime the preacher would say "freedom," I would bolt upright up in my chair, as though he had called my name. I always loved and resonated with the word freedom. As it turned out, freedom was all I ever wanted. Growing up, I felt controlled, restricted, and all I wanted was to be free. This strong desire for freedom governed my choices and actions for many years.

I loved and cherished the concept of freedom, but freedom didn't come easy or early in my life. I had to take myself through a restrictive and controlling childhood, an abusive marriage, and a near suicide before I found my way. I didn't come to have an awareness of anything resembling inner guidance until I was thirty-three.

You see, I wanted love and approval for as long as I can remember. My mother named me Frieda La Rue, and I never liked that name; actually, I despised it. As a little child, I honestly believed she didn't love me, and I thought naming me Frieda was proof. I was the youngest of six, one of two girls, and I chose to believe my mother favored my sister over me. Without knowing it, I created all kinds of unconscious drama to prove that to myself, despite her love for me. I lived my life motivated by the innocent yet limited perceptions that I developed as a child.

I wanted love and approval so badly that I married at sixteen just to get it. It would be years before I came to see how my early decisions were based on a need to get this adoration and to feel I was loved. This is not to say

I wasn't loved. I simply didn't feel it or believe it. My parents were deeply religious and ruled the home with a heavy religious hand, and I always felt different from the other girls. I couldn't wear pants, so when I would sit up in the bleachers for a football game at school, the boys would be below the slats, looking up my dress. I didn't understand how my parents would prefer that boys look up my dress rather than let me wear pants. What mostly stood out was the hypocrisy. The church elders and even my own parents did not always follow the rules we were made to follow; after all, they were human. Yet to my young mind, this made no sense.

I wanted to escape, and I thought that by getting married, I would finally find the freedom I was craving. But what I didn't know was that I would take the strong belief that I needed someone else's love and approval with me, wherever I went and in all my early experiences. So, until I could release the deep belief that I needed the approval of others, there would be no escape, and certainly no freedom. It would take several more years before I learned that lesson. But at sixteen, I was ecstatic about getting married, because it moved me away from my restrictive parents and the little town in Oklahoma where I grew up, all the way to Tennessee, twelve driving hours away.

The marriage, as it turned out, was riddled with affairs and physical abuse, and it ended in divorce after eight years. Deeply depressed, I attempted to cover my deep-seated anxiety by living an accelerated pace, with late nights, hard work, intense partying, and men. Finally, exhausted, I moved back to Oklahoma. Not long after, I met a charming limousine driver and became pregnant. Still deeply depressed and on the brink of suicide, it finally took a dream to awaken me and the gift of my son to inspire me.

At this time, I was very sick with Epstein Barr virus, which manifested in my body as chronic fatigue. I had no energy, was lethargic and barely getting out of bed, and had low blood pressure as well as hypoglycemia; I was just a real mess. I had my baby, but I was living a lie. My parents and family thought I was married to my son's father, but I wasn't, and the lie was making me very ill. Being unmarried with a child was a grave sin to my parents, and I wasn't okay with the idea of not being married and creating that pain for them. So my baby's father and I lied and pretended we were married. The lies went on for three years, and I became sicker and sicker. I knew I would have to tell my family the truth or it would kill me. It was around this time that I had a very haunting dream. It was a dream that was very real and very vivid. It was a dream that wouldn't leave me alone. I thought about it day and night for a week. It shook me to the core and left me trembling, as if someone took me and rattled me.

My parents had a little house down on the lake, and the people who had owned the house before them were square dancers, so the front yard was paved for square dancing parties. It was lovely. They had a front porch, which was great for the grandkids. We could sit out on the porch, and the kids could ride their scooters and play. We could also park our cars there, as there was very little grass in the front yard.

In my dream, my mom was in a white Porsche. My son's father owned a white Porsche, and she was behind the wheel and my aunt was sitting in the passenger seat. My brothers and sister and dad, my nephews and nieces, and all my immediate family in front of the house surrounded them.

I was standing on the passenger side of the Porsche, talking to my mom and my aunt, and suddenly a truck, like a semi-truck, came between the car and the house. The truck ran over me. It felt so real with adrenaline and everything, and I was thinking, I'm dead. I realized that I was still thinking, so I looked down and I pinched my arms. Oh my God, I still exist! I still existed, so I looked in the car. They're going to be so happy to know I'm okay. It was as if they didn't notice anything. They were looking at me but making no response, nothing. I wanted a response, some kind of feedback from them, so I decapitated myself. I didn't go through the actual motions. My head was just gone and blood was gushing like a fountain out of my neck. I was headless and blood was running down the window in front of their eyes, and I was looking at them, thinking, This will get a response. Nothing. No response. Nothing.

The dream was so real that I knew it had some amazing significance. A dear friend immediately recognized what it meant. She said, "The Porsche represents ultimate status, and your mother is behind the wheel, in charge of the family." As she was talking, my thoughts were saying, Yes, yes, that's it. Everything she was saying was ringing true for me. "She represents the ultimate to you, the one in charge. You're going to sacrifice your life for your family's approval, and you are never going to get it. You'll die and will never get it. You'll never get their approval, even if you kill yourself." She stopped, gazed intently at me, and asked, "How long are you going to live your life that way?" Without hesitation, pause, or uncertainty, I said, "Six weeks."

Where did that come from? Immediately, an image flashed in my mind of me walking out of that little country town in Oklahoma, heading to Texas with my two-year-old son on my shoulders. Growing up, I lived in Oklahoma, one mile from the Texas border. As a little girl, I'd walk around our town and in my backyard, look over to Texas, and yearn to be there. I always knew, even as a child, that in Dallas my life would come together. I knew it even when I forgot it, married, and moved away. I always felt my life would work when I got there. When my friend asked me that question and I answered "Six weeks," it wasn't me who answered—certainly not in the sense that I thought it through or pondered the question. My heart and a deep sense of sureness is what answered her. It was clear like a snapshot, a still frame in my awareness. I felt a deep knowing inside. The vision of walking to Dallas with my son shone brightly within me like rays of sunlight beaming through dark clouds. It was 1988, and finally, at twenty-eight, I was on my path to freedom.

~~~~~~~~~~~~~~~~~~~~~~~~~~~~~~~

That was the beginning of a new life for me. Without consciously realizing it, I had followed a certainty, a knowing inside of me that filled me with the confidence to strike out on my own, take my small child, and see what lay ahead. I felt guided, although I wouldn't have known to use those words.

I had been willing to walk and sleep under a bridge to get to Texas, but as it turned out, it wasn't necessary. A friend called and asked if I would be interested in house-sitting for her while she and her husband traveled. Three hours from the time she called, I had thrown my stuff into a suitcase and was on the road to Dallas. I remember the excitement I felt when she and her husband finally pulled out of their driveway and I was left alone in their house, two days shy of the six weeks to "stop living my life that way." I threw my hands up in the air and said, "Okay, God, what do you want me to do? I'm ready to start my life now."

"Call the court reporting school."

Court reporting? After nine years, I had reached the sales director level at Mary Kay Cosmetics. I made a decent living and loved my work, but I was ready for a change; it no longer reached a deep calling that I could feel and sense but couldn't put my finger on. So, although I didn't know what I was ready for, I came home one day and threw my pink cases with the mirrors and cosmetic samples into the closet. I can still hear them clinking and rattling as if they represented the shattering of beliefs and concepts I had been clutching. First thing Monday morning, I called the court reporting school.

I felt a connection with the first person I spoke to, Jim, a recruiter for one of the schools. He invited me to join his weekly Course in Miracles[1] group. Being in those meetings was exciting, simply exhilarating. I had no idea what I was reading, yet the messages spoke to me in a way I couldn't frame into words. Back at my mother's house, while sick and depressed, I snuck metaphysical books into my bedroom like a teenage boy hiding pornographic magazines under his bed. I was thirsting for this stuff; I wanted the pain to end. Jim had an incredible library filled with books about the old people we talk about today—the Eastern spiritual masters, poets, and philosophers.

Two months after I began investigating court reporter training, Jim told me not to pursue it. "You are not cut out for this." He was right.

Around this time, I had lunch with a friend, and as we were leaving the restaurant, she picked up a stack of business cards some business networkers had left behind. Scanning, she came to one that read "One Brain,"[2] and she said flippantly, "I don't know what this is, but it sounds like I need one." She attended an introductory meeting and called the next day. "La Rue, this is what you're looking for to change your life." I could feel the truth of that statement. I felt it inside me, and I could hardly wait until the following week to go to this introductory meeting. A joy welled inside me like a little kid the night before Christmas about to burst with bubbly, giddy expectation.

Then There Were Two

I was the first one there. Eager with anticipation, I filled out a questionnaire that had on it ten true-or-false questions. It was similar to those quizzes in women's magazines. They go something like this: "True or False? You have sex more than three times a week. True or False? You would have an affair with your husband's best friend." I always lied on those. I liked to leave that type of magazine on my living room coffee table. I wanted to be sure that when guests flipped through and read my answers, they wouldn't think something was wrong with me, that I was flawed in some way. So I'd make up the answers. But at this meeting, when they handed out the questionnaire, I made a decision: this time I'd answer honestly.

When they asked for a volunteer, my hand shot in the air so fast, no one else had a chance. The woman leading the meeting told me to bring up the completed questionnaire. She said to the class, "We're going to use kinesiology to find the answers to these." I had no clue what she meant, but I thought, No problem. I've been honest. She gently held both my arms out in front of me and softly pressed as she asked each of the ten true-or-false questions on the questionnaire. She explained that if my arms held strong, it meant true, and if my arms released or weakened, it meant false. This was called muscle testing.

What happened next blew my mind. Muscle testing revealed I had nine out of ten answers wrong! Only one was right. How could that be? I answered each question truthfully. Right then, I realized there was a part of me I didn't know. All these years and I didn't know who I was. I stood in front of fifteen people, yet in that moment, they seemed to evaporate. There was stillness. Awareness flooded in with specific memories of the times in my life when I firmly believed, "This project will work," or "I'm doing the right thing this time." Then, I'd embark on this right thing, sabotage myself, and become sick with failure. This was a light-bulb moment, a flash of insight as I realized there were at least two of me. The things I thought I believed were not the ones I really believed. There was a conscious self, the one I'm consciously aware of, and an unconscious self, which I had no idea existed—and they were not aligned. No wonder my life was spinning in circles. I was shocked. And I was excited. This process was a way to align those two parts of me—the conscious and unconscious selves—so we could work together in harmony. (See Appendix C: More about Evo-K)

The Closet

Using muscle testing, the workshop facilitator asked for my biggest block, the issue, she said, that needed to be dealt with right now. She went through a chart that listed a variety of issues. Mine turned out to be rejection. I had been in sales for nine years, and I knew rejection was spot on. I had become more suicidal, more fake, and more afraid. I was really shy and really scared, and the more rejection I faced, the worse it became. Sometimes, I felt like I was drowning in a sea of rejection. I tried to fake it, pretend it away, but the abyss had widened, and these feelings of shyness and fear had intensified. Yet, as it turned out, it wasn't my job in sales that caused this deep fear of rejection.

The woman placed her hands on my head, one hand on my forehead and the other on the back of my head, near my neck. Within moments, a memory arose. I was alone with my mother in the kitchen, and I had made something for her, scribbled on a piece of paper. I took it to her to show her. At two years old, I wanted a connection, and I was excited to show her what I had made for her. My mother was often in her own world. She was physically there, doing the motherly things, making sure we had clean clothes, food, and so forth, but there was no bonding, no sweet words of endearment. I said, "Mommy, look at what I made for you." She didn't look; she muttered, "Uh huh." I looked up and started to cry, but by the age of two, I had already learned you were not supposed to express tears, so I pushed them back. There I was, in front of fifteen people, recalling this memory. In my memory, I said, "But, Mommy, you didn't even look at it." She said, "Uh huh, it's nice; go put it up." So, I went into her bedroom, climbed on the dresser in the closet, and hid this paper with scribbles on it behind the blankets. Unconsciously, I locked my heart in the closet that day.

I had dreams about that closet for years. I didn't know why until that memory showed up. I realized how I began believing that who I was—what I had to offer—was of no value. If my own mother didn't want to look at my drawing, then to this two-year-old, what I have to offer is of no value;

something is wrong with me. The paper with the scratches and scribbles was me; it was me I put in the closet. My innocent little mind believed my mother didn't value me, and I thought I needed her to value me. Both my mother and I were innocent. It was at that workshop, at the age of twenty-nine, that I realized how I was still two years old.

I couldn't believe I had forgotten that experience for twenty-seven years. The memory was as real when it popped in, while standing in front of the class, as the day it happened. This was truly phenomenal. The woman asked, "If you could change this, how would you change it?" She explained, "The unconscious mind doesn't know the difference between what is real or imagined, so if you change a picture in your mind by imagining something different, it accepts it as true." She continued, "You can't change the past, but you can change how you feel about the past, the way you perceive it."

It took several minutes before I could come up with how I would change it. I wanted my mom to stop what she was doing and to look me in my eyes. I imagined her gazing at me with warm tenderness, connecting with me and making me feel special. Then something shifted. It was really me needing acknowledgment of my existence and value, and in that moment, I gave that acknowledgment back to me.

Over the years, there was much more internal processing to do, more work to come. It was just the beginning, but I felt okay. I was going to be all right after that.

The Prophet and the Phone Call

Many people influenced and traveled this path with me, but no one was more influential than a chiropractor I met in 1989 during one of his presentations.

Dr. John F. Demartini[3] was giving a lecture at Parker College in Dallas, Texas, when I first saw him. He mesmerized me, and during a break, after everyone else left the room, I was glued to my seat. I was frozen in place, unable to move. Dr. DeMartini walked back and forth on the stage, preparing for the second half of his talk, and noticed I was sitting there in the front row. He said to me, "I'm no psychic, but I am a prophet, and I can see you will go on to influence countless people."

Wow! Me? How can that be possible? His words touched a deep place in me. Have you ever had words spoken to you that go so deep within you that you have never forgotten them? I am not talking about hurtful or abusive comments, which seem to linger. I'm talking about words that so inspired and lifted you that, even without concrete evidence of their truthfulness, you felt such a deep resonance with them that you knew they were truth? That's how I felt. Even without evidence that I would, or even could, influence so many people, those words touched an area of possibility. The potential of it came alive. I sensed this man knew me at a far deeper level than I knew myself. I was certain, given the opportunity, that I would take one of his workshops.

After that astounding introductory class where I was introduced to kinesiology, I signed up for the training and became a certified practitioner. So, by the time I trained with Dr. Demartini, I had been doing personal coaching for a couple of years, helping people remove unconscious mental barriers. Yet even with these tools and their remarkable benefits in my life, I believed that once the brain and body died, I died. It was scary to think about dying. I was a body—to my mind, no more body meant no more me.

It was around this time a bizarre phenomenon began. I would hear my home phone ringing no matter where I was. I could be in California, and the ringing was just as clear as if I was at home in Texas. I would hear my phone ringing while shopping in a grocery store, or when I traveled out of state, or when I was in my office. I could hear my home phone ringing clearly, as though it was next to me and I could reach over, pick it up, and answer it. I didn't know what to think about this, and I didn't talk about it or tell anyone. Truly, what do you say to someone about this? It was just something I noticed. This bizarre phenomenon continued for six months. That's when I landed in Dr. John Demartini's workshop, a course teaching how to experience presence and joy, and how to connect to your soul.

I was born in a very strict, religious family, who passed along their ideologies of spirit and soul. As a little girl, I had been taught that I would either go to heaven or hell. Growing up, I couldn't grasp or understand what that meant, so I simply believed in a heaven and a hell, a spirit and soul.

Although I had been in the personal development field for a few years, workshops like this one were still pretty new to me. In this class, after we had gone through various processes, which seemed strange and foreign, Dr. Demartini said, "Now, I'm going to teach you how to listen to your soul." He led us through several rigorous breathing exercises, and at one point, we had to keep our eyes looking straight up, all the while breathing quite heavily. I thought I was going to hyperventilate and fall over. Then he said, "Put your attention on your heart—on your soul—and ask it what it wants you to know."

I expected nothing. I went through the motions, being very flippant about the whole thing. I remember thinking; I'm about dying here from breathing so hard. Finally, I put my attention on my heart. So, all right, what do you want me know? Unexpectedly and very suddenly, this voice spoke. It sounded just like my audible voice, except it was silent, soft, and very distinct. It rose from inside my heart and whispered, "I've been calling … and you haven't answered."

Oh my! I flashed back to the phone ringing phenomenon that occurred during those past six months. Images of the phone ringing flooded my memory. Could it be that the phone ringing was my soul calling? Was that possible? I was awed and so moved that I sobbed uncontrollably. It stirred very deep in my being in that moment. Everything in the room faded. The walls faded, and the people around blurred and receded into the background. The world inside me shifted. I didn't know I could have a dialogue with myself like that. I had conversations and arguments with my personality self—what I thought was my brain or conscience—but I didn't know I could talk to a wise self, a spiritual part of me. And I certainly didn't know this wise self could speak directly to me.

Silently, within, I asked, "I can talk with you?"

Silently, within, it answered, "I am always here for you."

It was on that day, in Dr. Demartini's workshop, that I made the conscious connection that I could communicate with the soul. It's been there my whole life. It told me to go to Dallas. It told me to call the court reporting school. That's when I met a man who exposed me to another world and ultimately led me to explore that other world. It told me to go to the One Brain introductory meeting and to pursue training in kinesiology. When I was on the brink of suicide, it told me to live for my son.

I didn't know that's what it was. I didn't know it was my soul. And although this experience moved me to tears, it still didn't seem possible. So it would be a while before I trusted its guidance and followed its direction. But it was a start.

At some point in my childhood, I found out La Rue was French. We had only three books in my house: a dictionary, a condensed encyclopedia, and the Bible. No other books came into our house, because due to my family's religious orientation, other books were feared to be evil. So somewhere, I looked la rue up, and was intrigued that it was French, which sounded so exotic. I learned it meant "the street" or "the avenue." Now, I have my own interpretation: "the path" or "the way"—the way to freedom. I liked La Rue, and eventually I forgave my mother for naming me Frieda.

SECTION ONE

Recognizing Your Essential Whisper

CHAPTER 1

✦ God by Any Other Name ✦

Your Essential Whisper

What would happen if we dropped the labels?

When something is labeled, it is defined and limited by the language and the culture of that language. Labeling anything pulls it from the background of oneness and separates it out. These labels become our reality. We define, limit, and name the reality we experience. And this is all just fine—really it is. Language and words allow us communication with one another. But, somewhere along the way, we have come to believe that our definition of something is what it is. We have come to believe that the word for something justifies its separation from everything else. We see a tree and consider it separate and disconnected from the air and the water and our breath.

We name our essence God, pull it out from our being, and separate it from what we are. As God sits in our imagination as a separate and distinct entity, we have to look outside our being for communication with it. We sit *it*—our idea of God— on alters and we pray to it. We hold *it* in temples to worship it. We have defined God through our various religions, rules, and dogma, and now, because of those definitions, *it* has to appear outside of us. God has been labeled, dissected, defined, and disconnected. Is it any wonder we have difficulty hearing the voice of God? And yet the distinct voice of God arises within, completely connected and easy to recognize, once we stop looking somewhere else. So call it what you are most comfortable calling it, but know this: you have always experienced its distinct communication and its abiding love, by whatever name you have given it.

The Golden Thread

Memories of what I perceived as painful situations no longer hold the emotional charge and angst they once did. As I tell these stories, I can see the golden thread that connects each moment, each frame of experience, to another and then to another and another, and so on. Nothing is wasted. No experience is unnecessary or worthless. The stories are simply the passage of this event and then another event, each with its distinct message, an unbreakable connection to the divine.

Growing up, we went to church every Sunday morning, every Sunday night, and every Wednesday night. Revivals happened frequently in that small town, during which we went to church every day of the week for a week or two. Visitors would come into town from all the surrounding counties. To me, the church was a scary place. People would speak in tongues. They'd speak in an unknown language, and it was followed by this hush ... complete stillness and silence. Then some authority would interpret the foreign language into English. I was just a child, and that's the way it seemed to me. One occasion, after we left the church revival, my mom would turn to my dad in the car on the way home and say, "That wa'nt God talkin'." It was eerie. Something about that didn't feel right to me. When I married at sixteen and walked out of that church, I was giddy with excitement. On the last Sunday I was there, I thought, I'll never go back there. Thank God I'm finally free from this! *That was in 1976.*

Thirty years later, in 2006, I went to church with my mother on Mother's Day. It was amazing. I no longer felt any judgment. The experience was simply beautiful and very pleasant. The church was in a different building in a different location with different people, but the religion was the same religion. This time, it was observed by different eyes. I was moved. I was touched. I could see the pure beauty in it, and the only thing that ever kept me from seeing that beauty before was my own judgment of it. My mother's way wasn't my path, but it had something to teach me.

When I visited my mother's church, the memories of that distant church—the church I found eerie, distasteful, and strange—had changed. I understood the beauty of it, the necessity of it, and its place in my life. So did the past change? Yes. The new experience changed the perception of the past, just as it changed in my two-year-old mind when I wanted that connection from my mother and ultimately gave it to myself. Presence releases the past. In any given moment, the past falls away. Today, I connect with Mom, my dear, sweet, eighty-six-year-old mother. Is she warmer, less formal, more embracing? No. She is exactly who she is today, as always. I just don't need her to be different, because I no longer carry the perceived need for her love and approval. The other voice of need and fear no longer blocks the warmth, closeness, and hugs I now have with her. It is very sweet.

Now when I ask, "Okay, God, what do you want me to do?" I know an answer will come, just as it did when it told me to call the court reporting schools. Once I realized I could get answers, I began to recognize the distinctive way they came in. There is a quality to this communication that is easily recognizable in the stories

Stories are doorways to our own recognition of the connecting points in our life. Memories revealed and reviewed as pure guidance have something to teach us. Very simply, there are no mistakes. It seems we live in a flow, a continuous flow of time, yet we really live in frames. *Snap, snap, snap.* Our perception of time and space gives us the illusion of life as a continuum, one long event. But is that true?

You have always received an answer to your deepest longings and your heartfelt questions. To recognize answers, however, requires willingness to open and receive this communication, so until you do, you may believe you are unable to get clear, direct communication. It is not the willingness that stands in the way for many, however; it is the ability to recognize the communication. In fact, you have received communication from the Whisper all along but perhaps called it something else. Once you discern these sensations and experiences as inner guidance, you will find it easier and easier to dialogue with this wisdom.

> **With practice and deliberate intention, dialoguing with your Whisper will become second nature to you. In truth, it is your real nature, your first nature.**

The Six Distinct Experiences

There are Six Distinct Experiences, and chances are you have experienced all six. It is within these experiences that you will find the sensations of the Whisper, what we call the voice of inner guidance. Why do we call these *distinct* experiences? For one, they generally occur quite outside of any deliberate intention to make them happen; these experiences seem to just show up. Secondly, these experiences don't feel like any of the normal day-to-day routines and activities. Distinctive in character and arising from your internal wisdom, these qualities of intuition are recognized as specific sensations and inner feelings.

The voice of the Whisper is undeniable. It is totally different from anything else. It is totally distinct from what we know as mind chatter, our incessant stream of thoughts. Sometimes we are afraid to follow what feels like inner guidance or an intuitive hunch. We tell ourselves it might not be our inner voice, and guess what? We may be right. There are feelings and thoughts that can convince you that you are listening to inner guidance. This is why distinctions are critical.

Distinctive in character and arising from your internal wisdom, these qualities are revealed as specific sensations and inner feelings of peace, sureness, energy, and joy. These sensations are recognizable through specific events and occurrences in our life experiences. The ability to make a distinction is vital in this. Clarifying these distinctions allows us to separate out the noise of our thoughts from the loving Whisper of our heart. But don't worry; you will get very clear, very quickly on the difference between the voice of guidance and the voice of disguise.

This distinct group of sensations is what we mean when we say *voice*. These sensations are the signature of your essential Whisper. We have located Six Distinct Ways, six events and circumstances, these sensations occur and can be felt.

- **Snapshot Click:** A time in your memory that is frozen, stilled, captured, and highly significant to you. When its significance is recognized or revealed to you, then it *clicks*.

   o *The Sensations:* High level of presence and awareness.

- **Collapsed Time and Space:** The experience of time slowing down or speeding up during a significant event and/or the experience of space expanding or contracting.

   o *The Sensations:* Expansion and openness, movement of time and space.

- **Urge:** The intense motivation to take a certain action without knowing why.

   o *The Sensations:* High level of energy to move; clarity of direction.

- **Wonderment:** The state of amazement and heightened awareness that occurs when your questions have been answered in a surprising and delightful way

  o *The Sensations:* Certainty and sureness; wonder and awe.

- **Knowing:** The full presence of alignment and certainty.

  o *The Sensations:* Certainty, resonance.

- **Inspiration:** The experience of intense energy to create.

  o *The Sensations:* High level of energy.

Did you recognize any of these? These Six Distinct Ways, when they show up, are united with qualities of spaciousness—a non-linear quality of inner stillness and a state of presence.

When these inner feelings and sensations occur, you are being prompted by your Essential Whisper to pay attention. These six experiences let you know that in that moment, you are connected to your soul, your highest voice, your Essential Whisper. These significant events are always accompanied by heightened awareness. These moments of heightened awareness are very distinctive in their qualities from the normal day-to-day activities, memories, and experiences. They are highly meaningful, highly significant, and easily recalled.

Once you recognize and are fully familiar with the sensations of your Essential Whisper, you will notice it rises and speaks to you continuously. You will find it easier and easier to understand and follow this wisdom once you discern this distinctive voice, this voice of inner God-self. Sometimes, these experiences will seem miraculous and perhaps otherworldly, and something that only someone else can do. Have you told yourself that hearing your inner voice is for special people with more intuitive skills or deserving dispositions? It is not true that receiving, trusting, and following your Essential Whisper is for other people. Your Whisper is not something outside of you; it's a direct line to your essential being, and we are all hooked up.

Recognizing the Whisper is more than just becoming familiar with the sensations of its voice; it's about recognizing the opportunities when they come to you, recognizing the answers to the questions you ask, and recognizing how simply wondering about something magnetizes the responses. To recognize is to know again—to remember the ancient song of your heart.

Now, let's take a closer look at each of these Six Distinct Ways to recognize inner guidance.

CHAPTER 2

The First Distinct Experience

✤ Snapshot Click ✦

The Bookmarks in Your Life

Snapshots are fragments of time woven throughout your life's story that will stand out to you as though a picture was taken of the moment. These significant pieces of time are distinctive connecting points in your story, threading individual messages of guidance throughout your life. In these brief and concise periods of time, generally no more than a few moments, you perceive the peculiarity of something as it occurs; perhaps it is a spoken word or phrase, or perhaps your attention is riveted on some detail of the unfolding scene. The event or situation feels significant to you, and your memory of it is clear and sharp.

You may notice as you recall a snapshot that you can't remember what was happening around you. The snapshot moment itself remains clear, while the surrounding scene and events appear to recede, fade, or blur. Reminiscent of a movie during a turning point in the storyline, the camera shot zooms in on the main characters for a close-up of the significant scene and blurs everything else in the background. This technique shows the audience that this moment in the story is critical; it tells the audience to pay attention.

Snapshots are like that. They are messages telling you to pay attention, to notice that this moment is a significant one in the movie of your life. The significance of these experiences is sensed and felt within, regardless of whether you know why it's important. The instant you do comprehend the significance of this distinct experience, you've received the *click*.

The Click

There's the story of a woman who worked in a hospital. One of her male patients watched a courtroom television show every day, without fail. One day, he remarked in passing, "Did you know that next to Oprah, Judge Judy makes more money than any woman on television?" This piece of trivia seemed important and captured her attention, so she remembered the comment. Not long after, this same woman became a contestant on a game show. She ultimately won the contest by getting to the next round by answering the question, "Next to Oprah Winfrey, what woman on television makes the most money?" *Snap. Click.*

When you uncover a snapshot and recognize the feeling of importance in your life, it is typically at a time when you are ready to understand the meaning given to you in the message. Recognition is sensed and felt as an "Aha!" a realization or a revelation. You are lit with insight, and this experience shifts your whole being; you are aware that something once hidden is now revealed. Suddenly, you understand how the snapshot is significant. "I get it!" Something in you *clicks*. **Snap. Click.** You have just heard from the Whisper. You may wonder how a simple memory, even if it is important, can possibly be the Whisper. How does the memory of a snapshot differ from any other memory?

Is It Real or Is It Memorex™?

If you're old enough, you may recall the popular television commercial that made the heading above famous. The sound quality on Memorex tapes was so clear, according to the advertisement, that one couldn't tell the difference between the taped version of a singing voice and an actual live singing voice.

Memories are a lot like that. What you consider as memory is the taped version. It feels real. It seems real. But is it? You already know memories are not always accurate. Have you ever recounted a story with a friend, and your friend said, "Well, that's not *exactly* how it happened." Or, certainly, you have heard funny tales of when a man attempts to retell a story about how he met his wife, and she snaps, "Honey, the dress I was wearing was blue, not red!"

What we remember is what we perceived happened. We put our spin on it. We determine what something means to us. A memory becomes what we tell ourselves happened. In specific types of hypnosis or age regression, the client is induced to go back in time to a specific memory or event. In this state, the client's perceptions or interpretations of a memory are suspended. Interestingly, even an emotional past event is narrated as if by a reporter— objective, without drama.

Our perception is simply the way we see something based on our interpretation of past experiences. Without the interpretation that would judge an experience good or bad, right or wrong, we notice what is real.

In Presence Sits the Truth

The six experiences are distinctive in nature, because during these situations, you slip into presence, as if by grace. Snap-clicks tell *you* the truth, not the other way around. These memories stand out to you; they reveal something significant for your life. You are not interpreting them, and, in fact, you'll find it difficult to determine why this memory stands out. This is a fine distinction about Snapshot as well as all of the six experiences.

What exactly does this mean, "tells you the truth"? In Snapshot moments, you are thrust into total presence. Many people describe this sensation as "heightened awareness." Truth is revealed to you in this state of heightened awareness—what is known as *reality* or *what is*. Here, the filters of perception and belief drop away. The veil is lifted. You see in front of you what is actually there, without interpretation or judgment. In the moment that Snapshot occurs, you are highly attentive. The colors are sharper, the impressions are clearer, and the words spoken are vividly remembered and easily recalled.

In a Snapshot, there is a message for you, bookmarked in place, and held for you to come back to during some part of your life. Often, a Snapshot is forgotten until just the moment when its significance is revealed. That's when you might exclaim, "Oh my! I completely forgot about that. So that's why *that* happened."

When my soul said to me, "I am always here for you," I felt the profoundness of the message but not necessarily the truth of it—not yet. From that point on, my awareness of direct messages heightened, but I wasn't entirely convinced I had received those messages early in my life. How could that be? My life was filled with suffering. If my soul was talking to me back then, why didn't I hear it? Why didn't it stop my suffering and pain?

As time passed and I would ask these questions, Snapshots would arise. Moments of time frozen in my memory would pop up in response to these essential questions. One time I asked, "Why did you let me get married and suffer such abuse?" Within moments, I remembered clearly being asked by a friend, when I was sixteen and getting ready to marry, if this was what I really wanted to do. Immediately, I answered, "Of course!" But the snapshot revealed to me what I was really thinking. I wanted to get married to escape. This was my way out of that little town. I was ecstatic that I had a chance to legitimately leave. You see, people thought I was pregnant. I wasn't, but I let them believe I was so they would bless the marriage.

The Snapshot revealed to me the moment when my inner voice said, "You're lying." What did I know at sixteen about listening to a voice of wisdom? To me, that was just another thought keeping me from escaping. I believed it was my conscience trying to make me feel wrong or guilty. I wanted out, and if there was another way to freedom, to escape, I certainly couldn't see it. And anyway, he loved me, right?

My dream was to be a concert pianist or singer. In my early teens, while still living at home, I had my own band—gospel music of course, because it was the only kind of music we were allowed to sing. I was pretty well-known for singing in that little town of Jimtown, Oklahoma, and in all the little churches that spread throughout several counties. I was known as "the girl with the voice," so to my mind, I was the world's best singer. Then reality hit. I entered a singing competition, and the judges told me that my voice was caught in my throat. I never sang again. That was it, the end of singing. I thought they were telling me I couldn't sing. I didn't know to ask them, "What do I do about that?" or "How do I change that? What do I need to do to improve?"

I didn't sing until just a few years ago, when I started to sing aloud in the shower, around the house, and in the car. What did I know? When people told me things, I believed them. I simply didn't know to question what was true.

My boyfriend back then, the man I married, didn't want me to sing along with the radio when we were in the car together. He would turn the radio volume up so that he wouldn't have to hear me. He thought he was a much better singer than I was and told me so. He also told me I couldn't sing, so I acquiesced and shut up when he turned the volume up to drown me out. I believed him when he told me I couldn't sing. And I believed him when he told me he loved me.

These Snapshots opened me up to glimpse all the times in my early life, even back then, when I was guided and held in the arms of true love.

Snapshots reveal answers to your essential questions—the questions relevant to what you are going through right now. The answers seem to come forward from the past, but in truth, they simply wait for you to recognize them. Snapshots are so much fun to recall, and by now, you may have remembered some of your own. So, let's play with this a bit and see what shows up for you. Take a few moments and find your Snapshot-Click by doing the following exercise.

FINDING YOUR WHISPER MOMENTS
When You Have Been Snapshot-Clicked

You won't have to work too hard at this. Any memory that stands out and is important to you is a Snapshot. Some examples of Snapshots are:

- When someone said something to you that felt was important or changed you in some way. You clearly remember the words spoken. If you were there with the individual, you may clearly remember the expression on the person's face.

- The moment you received a realization of something, a strong sense of presence, and/or a feeling of "Aha!"

- When you were given information or an idea that was different than or contrary to what you believed was true, and this idea stands out to you.

- Significant events in your life, such as giving birth, graduation, or receiving an award.

1) Locating the Snapshot
Write down the significant and specific details, not just the general memory. For example, if the memory of what someone said to you stands out, then write the words you heard and the images that are frozen, stilled, or vivid, such as the expressions on faces, the thoughts you had, and so on.

2) Locating the Click
Now, you want to locate the Click. Using the Snapshot you wrote about above, think about the click of recognition in this memory. What is it you now realize about this event or moment? How is the moment important to you?

3) Locating the Message
The Whisper speaks to us in these moments. What is your Whisper telling you? **Please don't censor this! Write what bubbles up from your heart**. Remember the Whisper does not criticize or negate us in any way. That only happens when we engage in analysis. Don't analyze! The message will arise naturally and spontaneously. What is the *essence* of your snapshot? If you cannot get a specific message, then place your attention on the sensations you felt at the time.

As you begin this process of recalling these Snapshots, you may find that throughout the day, several memories will spontaneously show up. Capture these because they are your connecting points. They are the guideposts in your life's story.

To explore Snapshots deeper, you may also go to Week One in the Eight-Week Practice Guide in Section Four.

There are a few journal pages located in the back of this book or you may download a complimentary copy of *Your Essential Whisper Journal* by going to http://www.ILoveMyWhisper.com

Snapshot: When I was in the fifth grade, my mom pulled me out of school to go see Yul Brynner in *The King and I*. As we were heading out the classroom door, my teacher, who was a very imposing six-foot-three-inch-tall woman old enough to be my mother's mother, said, "Some of us don't have time to go out and play. We have work to do." And my mom, who is *not* the queen of the comeback, fired back, "Some of us know what real education is."

Click: Recently, I was listening to a conference teleseminar call hosted by a trusted mentor. She was introducing us to an opportunity to be the pilot group, at greatly reduced cost, for a business/life coaching program. I loved the content and thought the interviewee was exactly the resource I needed, but I balked at the cost. I asked if there was a home-study version of the material at a lower cost. My mentor responded by telling the story of how she really wanted to see Yul Brynner in *The King and I* and talked herself out of it because $50 was a gigantic amount of money in her world. Six months later, he died, and she's regretted her decision ever since. I got chills and clicked my way over to the sign-up page.

Laurie Gennari, Redwood City, CA

Chapter 3

The Second Distinct Experience

✦ Collapsed Time and Space ✦

The Eternal

Collapsed Time and Space is a distinct experience that busts the rules about time and space. Time and space, normally considered and experienced as sequential and solid, instead feel fluid, spacious, and expansive during this type of event. Similar to Snapshot, the surroundings seem to fade or recede into the background, while the significant event or experience is heightened and singled out. However, during these events, there is a distinct sense of movement felt as opposed to the still photograph quality of a Snapshot.

The sensations of Collapsed Time and of Collapsed Space are similar, but it may be easier for you to remember your experiences of these situations if they are reviewed and considered individually. First, let's cover Collapsed Time.

There are two types of Collapsed Time:

1. Time slows down
2. Time speeds up

Time Seems to Slow Down

This type of Collapsed Time is when you experience an event as though in slow motion. You remember the details of the situation; you have ample time to take it all in and process it, yet the event happens very quickly. You can perfectly recall the colors, sights, sounds, and even smells. These details are clear and vivid.

Many people have felt this *collapsing of time* during a disturbing or traumatic experience, such as a car accident. The collision took only seconds, yet each aspect of the accident is recalled in minute detail, as though the event stretched several minutes or longer. Amazingly, even thoughts and impressions are remembered with ease. The event, not always felt or experienced in slow motion, upon recall has a spacious quality and *stillness* that was felt during the episode.

Time Seems to Speed Up

This is when events seem to speed up, breaking the rules and beliefs of how long something should take. Most often, this occurs during periods of intense concentration and absorption on a project or task. You look up from your work and think, *Time went by so fast. I wonder where the time went.* Begin paying attention to these shifts in your perception of time.

~~~~~~~~~~~~~~~~~~~~~~~~~~

I was in a car accident, and although it was minor, it really stands out for me. I drove into town, and I remember looking down at the speedometer and seeing my speed at fifty mph. It is interesting I remember that. I wonder if, at that moment, I was being told to slow down. The road curved up and to the right and then back down to the left, and just over the top was a driveway to the left; on the right was a ravine several feet lower than the road. As I topped the hill, directly in front of me was a car stopped behind a school bus. The bus was waiting to make the left turn into the driveway to drop off some children. I remember seeing kids standing up in the back of the bus and looking at me with their mouths open, because they could see I was about to collide with the car that was stopped behind the bus.

This happened in slow motion; it was as though time stopped. I had a choice. If I went to the right, the car might roll into the ravine. I could see in my mind the car floating off to the right, into the ditch. Or I could stop and collide into the car in front of me. I couldn't go to the left, because there was oncoming traffic. It seemed I had all the time in the world to think about my choices and select one.

I chose to hit my breaks as fast as I could. I plowed into the stopped car in front of me. The moment I slammed into the car, the bus miraculously turned, which prevented the car I hit from colliding with it. What I remember is that time stood still; there was no such thing as time. This happened in seconds, yet it seemed as if I had forever to make up my mind about what to do.

What really stands out is there was no feeling of fear. It was an eternal moment. I was young, and at that time in my life, I thought I was a physical being in a body. This experience showed me another aspect of my being.

We get to witness the eternal in experiences of Collapsed Time. We get to glimpse something other than our illusions and concepts of time.

An endearing man shared how he had plummeted five stories to the ground. He recalled, with almost frightening detail, the thoughts, actions, and decisions he made while he was falling. The specifics and description he relayed was amazingly vivid for an event that probably took five seconds. What he remembered most was the peace. He said, "I felt eternal."

The Concept of Time

We manage our life by the clock. We develop our schedules, plans, meals, and even our bathroom breaks according to what time it is. We have appointments, meetings, time frames, and deadlines. From the moment we are born, we are told what to do when. It is rare, in our daily lives, that we follow the natural flow of energy, eating when hungry, rising when awake, or resting when weary. Instead, alarm clocks startle us awake at designated times, and we sit in rush-hour traffic, hurrying get someplace on time.

How might your life be different if the thought to do the dishes immediately and even simultaneously moved the body to do the dishes? Thought and body as one. The thought to get a drink of water moves the body to get a drink of water. The thought to rise when you awaken moves the body out of bed. What would your life be like if you moved only when, and as, you were guided?

Have you ever heard the concept that time is a construct of mind or that time is an illusion? Without a direct experience of time shifting or falling away, any concept touting that time is an illusion would have to seem like pretty heady stuff. Experiences of Collapsed Time give us a glimpse into the ephemeral quality of time. Time becomes less rigid and definable, and instead becomes, at least to our senses, open to creation.

Here's a way to give you an experience of this. Think about what you were doing five minutes ago. Notice that to do this, you construct an image or picture in your mind of what you were doing then. *Then,* however, no longer exists. What remains are your memories about *then.* You are constructing the past within your mind, and even doing this becomes the past. Oops, it's gone.

Now, imagine what you will be doing in five minutes, perhaps still reading this book, or perhaps you see yourself moving to another activity. Notice how you use the same faculties of mind to imagine the future as you did to recall the past. This is how we form the past and the future. Other than our thoughts about the past or the future, the only existence (time) is *now*. Collapsed Time gives us a peek into timelessness—an experience of a fearless now.

Collapsed Space

Collapsed Space is similar to Collapsed Time, as this unique experience breaks the rules about space. The space or environment you are in seems to move—shift in size or appearance—contract, or expand. Once again, the significant action pulls forward and sharpens, while the background around you recedes or disappears.

There's another type of movie scene that makes for a good example. This one depicts the main character standing or walking along a long corridor or stretch of land. At the end of this corridor or destination, there is an ominous or threatening confrontation this character has to face. The camera zooms out, and the distance seems to stretch to infinity, giving the impression that twenty feet is more like one hundred and twenty feet. Westerns famously portray scenes in which two cowboys have to face off as they walk toward one another for the shootout. A distance that should take only a few seconds to walk takes minutes. Common in movies, this type of filming highlights that the character is nervous or anxious about what is to come, yet he moves forward courageously. This is what it feels like when space collapses. The space around you seems flexible and moving.

From Vanessa: *A situation like this occurred while I was a nursing student in college and studying psychiatric nursing at the Rhode Island State Mental Institution. Back in the seventies, these types of facilities were common. Each student was assigned a patient to work with. Mine was a twenty-two-year-old female, the same age as I was. She was diagnosed as a paranoid schizophrenic, and I had no idea what to do. After several weeks, however, I became quite fond of her. Fortunately, we had a wise nursing instructor, who on our last day at the facility gave us a stern lecture about saying good-bye to our patients. She admonished, "Not 'So long,' not 'I'll write you,' not 'I'll come and visit,' but, 'Good-bye.'" She led us through a Gestalt process—a deep visualization—that would help us to do this by pulling up a memory of someone we hadn't said good-bye to but wished we had.*

When I left that day for the final time, the walk down the corridor to the exit door seemed to stretch to infinity. I can still hear my footsteps on the linoleum floor and feel my patient's eyes boring into the back of my head. I dared not turn around. I walked on, and the walls on both sides seemed to move, undulating in and out; and the exit, instead of getting closer, seemed to get farther away. Finally, I reached the massive metal door and beckoned the guard to open it. As soon as I was on the other side of the entry, time and space shifted back into place. I got a real taste of what it means to say good-bye. I was no longer afraid of good-byes.

So what is solid? Are the walls solid? Does space move? Science now tells us that all objects move. At the quantum level, physicists claim there is more space between particles than there are particles, and that there is a constant exchange of energy and movement. An experience of Collapsed Space, similar to Collapsed Time, places us in a high state of presence, because what our beliefs have determined is that the rules about time and space no longer apply. **There are no rules in presence.**

Your inner sensations, your Whisper, reveal to you that something significant is occurring that otherwise would remain hidden. You notice *what is* in the moment. When you experience or remember Collapsed Time and Space, look at these noteworthy instances with new eyes. Find out what the high level of awareness and the sense of heightened presence are telling you.

FINDING YOUR WHISPER MOMENTS
Locating Collapsed Time

Can you think of a memory of Collapsed Time or Space?

Can you feel the sensation of presence in those moments?

Many people who have had near-death or traumatic experiences say that in the moment when time slowed down, they experienced tremendous peace and a feeling of well-being. There was no fear. Perhaps the message to these people is "There is nothing to fear, even death." To hear your Whisper's message, place your attention on the element in your memory that stands out the most—on the moment of *stillness within the movement.* Stay with that memory for a few moments. What sensations do you recall? What impressions or thoughts do you remember? Write these down and pay particular attention to the sensations and feelings.

TRY THIS:

CHOOSE ONE HOUR THIS WEEK WHEN YOU WILL FOLLOW THE ENERGY OF YOUR WHISPER AND NOT THE CLOCK

As you practice following the guidance of your Whisper—when you use your energy and the feelings of energy inside you to guide your actions—you will find you get much more done in your day, with minimal stress, without wasting time or worrying about time.

CHAPTER 4

The Third Distinct Experience

❧ Urge ❧

The Energy that Guides Your Next Step

Urge is recognized as heightened energy, along with a magnetic pull and a sudden inexplicable desire to do something. There is an immediate, usually impulsive energy that mysteriously moves your attention from what it was on to something else. The shift in attention linked with desire occurs for no apparent reason; however, there is the distinct sensation of certainty in what action to take. You know what to do even without a clue as to why.

The unique experience of urgency is not an emergency. An emergency is a critical situation that requires your immediate consideration, and the problem is *known* to you; you act or respond to a condition that you know needs your direct attention. Urge, on the other hand, is usually a spontaneous desire that captures your awareness and inspires energy toward a particular action, but you are not sure why. The energy of Urge is an internal sensation that motivates and stirs movement, and when the guidance of Urge is followed, the reason why that action was needed becomes apparent, although perhaps much later.

~~~~~~~~~~~~~~~~~~~~~~~~~

Back when I was a sales director living in South Carolina and recently divorced, I would hold weekly sales meetings at a newly built Holiday Inn with ballrooms, which for this small town was really quite lovely. I became good friends with the hotel sales director, Dorothy, and would join her and a group of her co-workers every Wednesday night. This was during the time when the TV show Star Search was popular. Each Wednesday at this hotel, they would have a Star Search contest, and they invited me to be a judge. One night, the group of us looked up and Dorothy was gone; she just disappeared. We asked around. Her car was gone, and no one knew where she was. Phone calls were made to her home the next day and the day after, and still no word from Dorothy. A few days later, she returned to work and explained, "I was just sitting there watching the show, and I knew my husband was in trouble. I had to go, and there was no time to say good-bye. I had to go, so I just left." She lived five or ten minutes from the hotel. When she arrived home, her husband was bent over the bathtub, vomiting blood. She rushed him to the hospital and ended up saving his life, because she followed the urge to go home.

I was so intrigued by that. How did she know? She was sitting there watching a show, and suddenly, urgently, she had to leave. I was fascinated by that for years.

When Someone Else's Whisper Urges Us

Have you ever had someone tell you, with utmost sincerity and conviction, that you should check out a specific job or profession or talk to a particular individual? The moment you heard those words, you felt them deeply inside as the truth and you felt moved to follow the advice.

The Urge to tell you something is different than a desire to give you an opinion. Often, the one giving you the information from an Urge doesn't realize its significance and may not even remember giving you the message. She simply followed the Urge to say something to you, perhaps for very different or personal reasons. The Urge to communicate something to someone has no manipulation in it at all. Messages prompted by Urge rise from the heart and are felt within as a desire to say or express something without knowing the value or significance to the other person.

Have you ever gone back to say thank you to someone who said something profound to you, and he didn't remember what he said to you? Or has someone come up to you, bubbling with gratitude over some message you gave, and you didn't have any idea what it was you conveyed? This is responding to an Urge with no personal agenda or awareness of the message's significance to the other person.

If someone acts on an Urge and gives you information or presses you to consider something, which perhaps steps outside your belief system or standard way of doing something, pay attention. It just may be *your Whisper* giving you advice on how to take your business, relationship, or ideas to the next level.

~~~~~~~~~~~~~~~~~~~~~~~~~~~~~~~~~

Much of my life direction happened through the urges of others—the heartfelt, compelling persuasion of other people moved me to explore their suggestions or advice. For example, I never set out to teach anything. I was simply planning to see my clients and live happily ever after. When people began asking me to teach classes, I would refuse. Eventually, I did start offering facilitator training and other classes, but I had no intention or desire to teach, and I had never taught a class without the insistence of others.

My friend Debbie, who had been receiving personal sessions with me in Dallas, married and moved to San Francisco. Off and on for three years, she'd call me and ask if I would do phone sessions with her. I had been taught that kinesiology could not be done on me as a surrogate, and so I believed I could not do sessions with clients unless they were face-to-face.

Debbie, however, was persistent and would constantly call to persuade me to do long-distance phone sessions with her. Despite her persistence, I sent her to the trainers I had studied under who lived within driving distance from her California home. After each visit to them, she would call and say, "La Rue, it just isn't the same. Would you please just try and do this for me?" I would reply that I couldn't, until one day I relented and said, "Debbie, I don't know if this is going to work or not, but I'll do the session for you."

The belief that I could not use muscle testing on myself and get accurate answers had been self-fulfilling. Up until then, I had no evidence or proof that enabled me to believe I could muscle test as a surrogate for a client and get accurate answers. When I would use the procedure on myself, sometimes the answers were accurate and sometimes they were not. I had no certainty and no conviction in using this process as a surrogate. I told Debbie that if it was effective for her, then she could pay me, and if it wasn't, then we would know and she could stop asking me to do phone sessions.

The very next day, she called and said, "La Rue, it was just as effective over the phone as in person." She experienced significant and positive changes as well as a profound shift in her relationship with her daughter, which until then had caused considerable stress. That's when I understood that my own beliefs about doing this work as a surrogate had kept me from exploring whether they were really true. Debbie's persistent Urge enabled me to gain another perspective in my work. My practice has exploded since then, and went national almost overnight, because there were people who had move away and wanted my help.

Currently, most of my client sessions are done by phone, with over 50 percent overseas. Previously, people had to live locally or travel to get in-person sessions. I told Debbie that her insistence on doing phone sessions changed the course and direction of my work, and interestingly, she was very surprised. She had no idea she played a pivotal role in the expansion of my practice and business.

Many people find the distinct experience of Urge to be the easiest to remember. You feel a quick and spontaneous desire to do something, yet you have no earthly idea why. These sensations are often hard to forget or ignore. An Urge is generally pressing and sharp, but occasionally it may feel more like a nudge—a gentle pull, a subtle movement of energy inspiring you to act on something. You can be nudged to go to the store, for example, when you don't have anything to buy, or to call someone to whom you haven't spoken in years.

From Vanessa: *At the grocery store one day, while scanning the spice aisle, I felt a nudge to get cream of tartar. I had no idea what cream of tartar was or how to use it. I picked it up, looked at it, and placed it back on the shelf. Moments later, my hand reached for it again. I felt moved to get it, but I also heard my thoughts questioning the action,* What is cream of tartar? You've never used that before. You're just imagining this. *Finally, the energy to get the small bottle of this white spice was too much, and I reasoned that the small cost was okay, even if I didn't use it. Three days later, I had the Urge to try a new recipe. It called for cream of tartar, one-eighth teaspoon.*

Did you follow the sensation of desire and energy? What happened as a result? In Urge, as in all Six Distinct Experiences, there is a sensation of certainty. You needed nothing at the store, or had no reason to make the call, yet the sensation felt certain and sure. This is what certainty feels like. Become familiar with it; get to know it again. Let it wash over you like a warm, inviting shower. Flow with it, and embrace it in your life.

FINDING YOUR WHISPER MOMENTS

Locating Urge

The sensation of desire and energy pulling you toward a particular action makes no sense logically. This is the big clue that you are experiencing an Urge.

What is your story? Find a time in your life when you felt a compelling Urge (or a subtle, certain nudge) to take some action. You did not know why, yet you followed it anyway. **Write your story here:**

What happened? How did it play out? Did this action lead you to another action? What opened up for you? **Write your experience(s) here:**

CHAPTER 5

The Fourth Distinct Experience

⤐ Wonderment ⤏

The Presence of Awe

Wonderment is the state of awe, and in this state, you sense you are in the presence of God. You asked a question, pondered a thought, or expressed curiosity or doubt about something, and you are amazed and surprised at the wondrous way your question has been answered. What you wanted to know, what you wondered about, is answered in an astonishing and unexpected way, filling you with revelation, enchantment, and unanticipated joy. This state of Wonderment acts as a direct answer from your soul to you.

Wonderment is an interesting experience in that it is prompted by a particular thought or question.

There are two types of questions that give rise to Wonderment:

1. Wondering

A wondering is a thought or question you have that arises spontaneously and that is curious, open, and receptive to an idea or an inspiration. "Hmmm … I wonder …"

2. The Essential Question

An essential question sparks dialogue with your Whisper. The essential question is the one that you are left with after you've exhausted trying to find your own answers to a problem or situation. Sometimes, it's the *down-and-out* question. Many people only ask this type of question after they have reached a low point in their life. These essential questions are the "I really want to know the truth" or "Please help me" kinds of questions.

> **In both wondering and essential questions, you have stopped trying to seek an answer or figure anything out.**

When you surrender what you think you know and intentionally move into "I don't know," you shift, automatically and easily, into the realm of unlimited potential. This is such a sweet, sweet place to be. You are open; you allow information to come to you and follow the sensations of guidance rather than hunt and seek for the answer. Your answers then arrive in surprising and illuminating ways.

~~~~~~~~~~~~~~~~~~~~~~~~~~~~

One day I wandered to my kitchen cabinet, looking for something where I keep my vitamins. The cabinet was filled with a plethora of supplements that I never take. I saw I needed a really good vitamin, and I didn't want to take endless bottles of capsules. It was just a really simple thought: I need to have really good stuff, because a lot of stuff they sell you is not even effective, and one supplement cancels out another. And then I went about my business.

This happened on a Wednesday or Thursday, and on Sunday I went to Starbucks. As I was sitting with my laptop to do some writing, this incredible energy walked through the door. I heard a young guy say, "Hey, Frank!" and he sat down and had a conversation with Frank, three or four tables over. I could hear every word, and I was intrigued by their conversation, because he was talking about the law of attraction, which he learned about the day before. I knew the authors they were talking about and thought, Oh I'd like to talk to him. Then I went back to writing and took my attention off them. About an hour or so later, I hear this man's voice next to me.

"Hey what'ya doing?" He was sitting in the chair next to me, facing me.

I responded, "I'm writing."

"What are you writing?" He leaned over, looking at my computer screen.

"I'm writing a book."

"Well, what are you writing about?"

"I'm writing about life."

"What? Tell me more. What do you do?"

Clearly, he wasn't going to go away. I invited him to join me, and during our conversation, I found out he sold "the world's greatest vitamin." Truly. He had with him a third-party consumer's report with endorsements from companies showing the effectiveness of these vitamins. He told me where I could get the consumer's report and how I could get the vitamins. There was my answer. I could take one easy package in the morning and one easy package at night.

Wondering about vitamins and wondering if there was a better way to take vitamins opened my awareness to recognize when vitamins showed up. Very likely, I would not have listened to this man talk to me about vitamins had I not been opened to noticing. When I wondered about finding a good vitamin that was convenient to take, the universe—something that appears to be separate from me and really isn't—responded and brought me vitamins ... right there at Starbucks.

FINDING YOUR WHISPER MOMENTS
Changing Worry to Wonder

Try This: Bring your thoughts to something you are afraid of or worried about happening. Be gentle and don't move too deeply into the worry. Simply think of a situation that you have some concern about and form a question around it. For example, say you are worried about your mom going to a nursing home. You might be asking, "What is she going to do? How will she get the medical help she needs? Why is she so resistant? Why isn't she taking this seriously?" Bring one question or two at most, to mind around what you are worried about. **Write them down here:**

Now, take several deep breaths. Repeat a couple of times, "I don't know the answer to this question." This is true, right? You don't know the answer, so stating this allows your mind to settle with that.

Placing your attention and your focus on your heart, change the question to an "I wonder if" statement. So, using the example above it might be "I wonder if Mom will find a suitable nursing home," or "I wonder how this will all turn out."
Write your wonder statement(s) here.

Can you feel the shift? Can you feel the difference between the worried question you wrote and your wonder statement? How would you describe the difference? Does it feel more open, receptive, and lighter? **Write what you feel here.**

Lately I have noticed that when I simply spontaneously wonder about something, the answer shows up without my even trying to figure out anything. The other day, I traveled over ten miles to my favorite barber. I keep my hair short, so I have a barber I have been using who does a fabulous job precision cutting my hair. I happen to like barbers, because they are accustomed to working on short hair. On this particular day, however, he wasn't there.

For a moment or two, I felt pretty bummed, as it is some distance from my house and I didn't know when I could make the trip again. Yet almost immediately, I relaxed and wondered, Hmmm, I wonder how I am going to get my hair cut. Then I went about my day.

Later that same day, I ran into a woman whose hairstyle I loved, and I asked her where she went to get it cut. She directed me to a barber she raved about—mind you, not a salon or hairdresser! And, as it turns out, this particular shop was only one mile from my house, not the ten I usually traveled! Well, long story short (excuse the pun) I love this barber! I got a fabulous cut.

The best part is, I simply wondered and released just like I learned in the Inner Advantage class! There was no struggle, no search through the Yellow Pages, and best of all, no worries. I just love listening to the Whisper!

Ronnis Oher, Chicago, IL

The I-Know-the-Answer Mind

Our mind responds to questions, and questions are powerful tools that lead us toward problem solving and cooperation. Ask yourself a question, any question, and the mind automatically and very quickly searches its data banks (memories, perceptions, experiences) for what it knows, and locates an answer. The thinking mind's job, its function, is to process information based on your beliefs, experiences, and the knowledge you have accumulated or continue to accumulate with research, query, discussion, and exploration. Typing these words uses this aspect of the mind. How and where to place the letters, the correct use of syntax, the occasional reference to the dictionary all use the brilliant processing of the rational mind as well as the emotional context of word placement to evoke images in the reader. Questions drive the entire process: what word to use here, what meaning to express there, what synonym to use that clarifies and illuminates precise meaning. In fact, it is a question—How can I tell the difference between the thoughts in my head and the voice in my heart?—that forms the entire basis, the foundational premise, of this book.

Questions are useful, there is no doubt; and even more significant, they are what drive most of our behaviors. What will I have for dinner? What should I wear today? What will the weather be like tomorrow? So the question to pose here is: When is it appropriate to employ analysis, research, study, and investigation, and when is it better to surrender to wonder? The answer: Allow the sensations of inner guidance to tell you how to get your answers. Suppose, for example, you have a strong desire and Urge (Third Distinct Experience) to go to the library and research the possible answers to a specific question. Go. Let your sensations tell you which librarian to approach and which resources to use, and when the energy leaves, leave.

If you feel a strong need to know something, to solve a problem a certain way by a certain time, then you will use considerable effort and concentration, and will generally struggle. This can lead to attachment—a strong need to know, figure it out, or get the right answer. Attached to the outcome, we search for the right answer, or justify the answer we've settled on. Whenever you have these strong emotional attachments to a particular outcome or result, that's the time to breathe, relax, and take your questions to wonder and place your attention on your inner sensations.

Here is an example of how an internal dialogue (thoughts) using the logical thinking mind we call the I-know-the-answer mind may have solved the problem of finding easy-to-take vitamins:
I need better vitamins. What kinds of vitamins should I take?
Perhaps I can stop at a health store and look around.
Well, I don't really have time today. Oh, let me look it up.
I remember someone mentioning that niacin was great for energy.
I really need some energy these days.
I didn't work out yesterday. Why do I always skip working out?
What is wrong with me? Don't I want to stay healthy?
Well, at least I am eating better.
Except for that toast I had this morning.
Well, don't I deserve a bit of strawberry jam?
Life is just no fun if there are too many restrictions.
Now where is that book on vitamins?
Wow, there are that many vitamins. How do you figure this out?
Why isn't there just a simple vitamin to take? This is nuts.
I'll call my friend. She'll be able to tell me.
And so on and so on …

Is this familiar? This is the thinking mind in action. This is not wrong. It is how the mind is structured, and its job is to get you an answer. Amazing in its ability to assess all of what you know or believe you know, the mind gives you evidence and proof supporting its conclusions. It's appropriate to engage in analysis for some things; it's simply not the only way.

Direct yourself another way to get your answers. Follow the sensations of guidance; tap into information that the I-know-the-answer mind does not have access to. The whole world and beyond is now available from which to draw your answer. From this place, this open and expansive state, life gets very, very exciting.

You can bypass analysis by asking genuine and sincere questions that arise from your heart—questions you really want the answers to—and then you ask to receive guidance. Curious and light-hearted wonderings as well as vital and essential questions have no attachment to time. There isn't a deadline; there isn't a particular outcome sought. You're simply asking with curious anticipation of what the answer could be. You're now open to all that is possible, and instead of chasing after what you want or searching endlessly, it is drawn to you.

Most significantly, these types of questions—wondering and essential—help you make the connections between what you ask for and what shows up as your answer.

Oh, by the way, LaRue brought Vitaman Man home with her, but you'll have to read on to get that story.

Essential Questions Surrender

The act of Wondering is non-linear in its quality and can often seem to appear out of nowhere. You are just wondering about something—although, as you've practiced in the exercise above, you can intentionally develop a Wondering. Wondering captures your attention and arises from your heart. You are prompted to open your awareness; you recognize your answers, because you remember having a curiosity about something.

Essential questions, on the other hand, are referred to as the down-and-out questions. They are described as down-and-out questions because many people don't ask these important and critical essential questions until they have exhausted other attempts to figure out their own answers, are helpless or hopeless, and have finally surrendered. Essential questions are yielding questions; they are critical questions that ask for the truth about something dear in your life. Although they can be intentionally invoked, not only when you hit a low point in your life, they are generally asked when you want guidance.

In the Finding Your Whisper Moments section above, you intentionally formulated a wondering statement or question. You can intentionally ask an essential question, as well, without being down and out, but you must really want to know the truth, your inner truth. *When you ask an essential question you are inviting a response from your Whisper, which just loves to answer you.* Your Whisper will answer your questions, yet you may not recognize the answer if you expect it to look a certain way. Wonderings and essential questions place you in an open state of receiving an answer from the sensations of guidance by suspending your beliefs that you already know the answer.

Examples of Essential Questions:

- *What is the best way for me to solve this problem?*
- *What is the next step for me to take toward my goal?*
- *How can I serve my soul's purpose today?*
- *What emotional memories do I still need to heal?*
- *What is it I feel most passionate about?*
- *What foods best serve my body today?*
- *Which decision holds the most joy for me?*
- *What Whispers have I been receiving?*
- *What simple step can I take to _____?*
- *What attracts me? What are my true desires?*
- *Who do I most need to forgive?*
- *Does what I want align with my true values?*
- *I'm tired of living my life this way. What do I need to do now?*
- *What resources do I have to help me reach my goals?*
- *How can I go after my dream right now?*
- *What is the best way for me to make more money doing what I love?*

Essential Questions Move You to Your Next Step

As you look over the list, do any questions stand out to you? Is there any question that you would like to receive an answer to because you have already tried to answer it over and over and haven't been able to? If so, keep in mind that an essential question is not a philosophical question about the meaning of life or the purpose of mankind. Although these are important and interesting questions, they are not considered essential to your well-being.

Your essential question is a question that asks what is necessary to take the next step; essential questions are vital to movement. To get unstuck in any area of your life requires movement and the willingness to take an action toward your heartfelt goal or idea. The essential-question leads to what is necessary for movement; you will receive an answer that will guide an action toward that next step. Take it.

Essential questions and curious wonderings open the way for answers to show up in amazing ways. Get ready to be awed.

One day I was feeling particularly sad about my life and current predicament. I had to find a job and was feeling that, despite my expensive college education and my degree in English, I was not adequately prepared for the very real task of finding a decent job. I had just spoken with a friend about this, and she said very clearly, possibly because she was tired of my endless whining, "Look, you have had tons of great opportunities in your life, but you are always so negative. You always find a reason not to accept these gifts when they come." I vehemently argued with what she had said. What did she know about me? I wasn't at all like that. At least that's what I thought. I saw myself as a very upbeat, optimistic, the-glass-is-half-full sort of person. So I knew she had me all wrong.

Nonetheless, that morning those words echoed inside of me and lingered. And even though I couldn't believe they were true, I felt as if something deep inside of me was trying to communicate with me, whispering to me to listen to those words closely with my heart and not my head. So I closed my eyes and felt as if I was having a conversation with this part of me deep inside. When I was still, I could hear it, just barely, like a hush or a whisper. Yet I didn't fully trust it. "Okay then," I said quite flippantly, "show me what you mean." Immediately, I had glimpses from my life—moments of hope and possibilities that never quite panned out and which I had never really recognized as opportunities.

This got my attention. I felt a question rise inside me: If you could have any job in the world, what would it be? I had asked myself this question so many times, but in this moment, I had a real response. I had just been to this Lasik clinic, and I loved the feeling of this place, the atmosphere, and the people there. They had been so kind to me and took me in the back after my boyfriend's surgery. At that point in my life, I could only dream of having the surgery, even though I really needed it. So I silently responded that I wanted to work at a place like the Mann Berkeley Caplan Laser Center. That answer was so clear, I surprised myself.

I had been scouting the newspaper that morning as part of my job search, and it was still open to the Office & Clerical Work section. I shifted my eyes from the Office & Clerical Work section to the Medical section, and to my utter surprise,

I came across the most beautifully written ad for a patient counselor at the Mann Berkeley Caplan Laser Center. I almost fell off the chair. Now this voice had my attention. At the same time, I was still unsure. There was also an ad for an administrative assistant, and I thought, maybe I should apply for that also, especially since I knew absolutely nothing about eyes or Lasik surgery. It felt as if my inner voice was having a little fit. I could hear it yelling—still as a whisper, but as if it was having a mini temper tantrum. No, no, no, no, no! Just apply for the one job.

So I applied for the position of patient counselor, and I felt a sense of confidence I had never known before. I knew it was my job. Sure enough, I received a call about a week later. Within a very short time, I was working at the laser center. My benefits included free surgery, and I received the salary I had suggested to myself when prompted by my inner voice. Several months later, I requested a pay raise, and within a week, I got exactly what I asked for. Friends of mine think I have good job karma or great luck. I know I have an inner advantage! I follow the voice and listen. In this arena of my life, I know it defies usual logic.

Erika M. Nelson, Ph.D. Providence Village, TX

CHAPTER 6

The Fifth Distinct Experience

✦ Knowing ✦

The Message of Resonance

Knowing is the experience of resonance. You recognize that what you know, felt through the internal energy of sureness and certainty, is spot on. This experience shifts your framework, perhaps your life's direction. A new course is open; a new path is chosen.

We each have an innate ability to sense what is called *resonance*. Perhaps you have said or have heard said, "This resonates with me." Resonance is a particular feeling of deep alignment. Some call this a *vibration*. At a certain level of existence, the quantum level, everything vibrates, moves, and exchanges energy, including thoughts, beliefs, and ideas. As it turns out, we are so much more than a physical body; we are vibrating essence. The essence of who we are is the highest nature of what we are; the vibration of our individualized essence is our highest level of being and energy, our intrinsic blueprint. Alignment occurs when what you desire matches in vibration with the expression of your essence. Knowing is the experience of feeling aligned; you feel aligned and on target at this moment in your life's journey.

Have you ever had the feeling that you know what you know? This is the state of Knowing, and it often comes on suddenly, even surprisingly, as the experience prompts a change in direction. You are in harmony with a decision you've made or a direction you plan to embark on. You feel and experience this Knowing in your being as absolute certainty with no doubt, and it literally fills you with confidence. Knowing may come with an urge to take action, or sometimes you get a Knowing and there is nothing else to do or decide.

~~~~~~~~~~~~~~~~~~~~

Emily is a beautiful woman who I worked with in sessions for about a year and who experienced deep shifts and transformation in her life. During one of our visits, she said to me, "LaRue, I see you in England, and one day I'm going to get you there to present this work." She was referring to the work I do in my private practice, from which she experienced profound changes. I felt her clarity and sincerity when she spoke, and in that moment, I had a Knowing that I would be in England. I could clearly see myself teaching classes there, and I knew in my being, with no doubt, that my work would expand to England.

No Urge came with this Knowing. There was no urge to do anything or take any action to get to England. About a year later, out of the blue, another woman, a mutual friend, asked that I join her at Emily's home in England. When I went there, I had no plans to discuss, offer, or present my work. I was simply going as a guest. Yet I had the Knowing that I would get the opportunity, and I didn't have to try to make that happen. As it turns out, Emily said, "Since you're in England, why don't we do an introductory event and invite people to experience your work?" That day, she sent out three hundred emails, and in two days, we had a room of fifty people.

~~~~~~~~~~~~~~~~~~~~~~~~~~~~~

Knowing, as a distinct experience, is unlike belief. With a belief, you know something because your experiences and perceptions support that belief and prove to you it is true. All of your beliefs will feel true to you, and, in fact, all your beliefs are true to you. You have all of the evidence to support and validate why you believe what you believe. You might even say, "I know it because …" and give all the reasons why you believe something. (This is discussed in greater depth in Chapter 11.) This is very different from the experience of Knowing with the sensations of resonance that arise without any firm foundation for knowing and without substantiated reasons or proof that support the Knowing.

Further, beliefs are often contradicted by other beliefs. Not with Knowing. You feel no internal conflict, no wavering or doubt, yet you are perplexed as to how you know what you do. Beliefs are often contradictory, and the strong desire to defend them arises if they are challenged. When you hold two or more opposing beliefs, you will feel this as stress in the body.

Here is an example of how we can hold in mind several opposing beliefs:

Belief one: I can never hold on to money.
Belief two: I should invest in real estate.
Belief three: It is too hard to learn something new.

Can you see the conflict in these? Let's take a closer look. If you believe that money is hard to hold on to, then other beliefs have to exist to support that. Some of these might be, "I can't save money" or "I never have enough money." Suppose you want to invest in real estate, and you have the belief you can't hold on to money or you never have enough money. What happens to the idea of investing? It would be very difficult to look at the options for investing, while you believe that you never have enough money. After all, where is the money coming from for the investment? These beliefs close off or limit the options and avenues for securing money, right?

Let's say you move beyond the first two beliefs and find a way to invest without a lot of money, but you have the belief that it is too hard to learn something new. Now what happens? Learning new investment strategies with this belief will definitely be difficult. These conflicting beliefs are stressful, and this is what makes changing so difficult for so many who truly desire to make changes in their lives. Yet, taken separately, each of these beliefs will feel true to the believer, regardless of their inherent contradiction.

The experience of Knowing produces no contradiction or conflict, because it is a deep, abiding truth that is being revealed to you. There is a clear distinction between the experience of Knowing and the feeling of belief. One way to distinguish between the two is that with Knowing, you don't know why or how you know; you just know. It feels cellular and organic, as if in the blood and bones. "I just know it in my bones." It is not mental, and furthermore, you are not about to be talked out of it. What is fascinating about Knowing is that even though you don't know why or how you know what you know, there are no feelings of stress, because the strong sensations of resonance and alignment override any conflicting thoughts or beliefs.

> **The sensation of Knowing shows you a different purpose than you thought you had. It shows you another way of doing something that, up to that moment, didn't occur to you as an option.**

The distinctive experience of Knowing points you in another direction, on another course, and it does so without doubt. It is built in, and you have arrived at a time and place in your life when you can recognize it.

~~~~~~~~~~~~~~~~~~~

When I left my hometown in Oklahoma, sick, suicidal, and with a baby, I knew I had to go to Dallas. Once I arrived, my heart instructed me to call the court reporting school. I thought I was to be a court reporter. Little did I understand that interviewing was simply the next step for me, and by going through the interview process, I would make a very important connection. One day, I was having lunch with a friend, and we noticed a business card left behind. So my friend decided to follow up on the information on the card. Two days later, she told me, "You have to go and do this! It will change your life."

As it turns out, it did change my life. That was when I was introduced to two of me. At that fateful introductory meeting, I knew I would do this work, and without hesitation, I dropped my belief that I would enroll in court reporting school. I had no idea how I would pay for the course or even if I could make a living; but I knew I would do this, and no one could talk me out of it. I knew that I knew that I knew. This Knowing led me in an entirely different and life-changing direction—even to this book you are reading. It never occurred to me in my wildest imaginings that I could go on to help others. After all, at that time, I could barely help myself, and yet Knowing pointed me on another course that felt sure and certain.

~~~~~~~~~~~~~~~~~~~

Warning and Foreboding

There is another kind of Knowing, as well. Have you ever felt foreboding and you knew something was wrong? You just knew someone was injured, hurt, or maybe had passed away. What was this feeling like for you? Some have described this as an *uncomfortable Knowing*, a strong sense of warning that something dire has occurred. Remember Dorothy, LaRue's friend, who felt an Urge to rush home, and when she arrived, found her husband very ill? She said later that she knew something was wrong. This is foreboding. The Urge gave her the tremendous energy to move quickly without knowing why, while the sensation of foreboding suppressed any thought to render the Urge invalid, which would have kept her from following it. Have you ever felt you were in danger and realized later that indeed you were? The sensation of foreboding acts as a warning, a signal to you, like a radar device or an alarm. Foreboding is a physical sensation that is manifested to warn you that someone or some situation needs your attention. Foreboding is the sensation that prompts you to pay attention to an inner message or gives you a lesson about what is occurring.

These situations of foreboding give us an opportunity to transform the limiting beliefs about danger, death, injury, or the wrongness of something into the light of love. Without foreboding, we wouldn't be able to sense the need to take a look at the fears that can grip us and keep us from evolving. Foreboding is the signal that a change within our belief system is coming. It enables us to prepare for what will be a significant lesson on the soul's journey. It is another opportunity for us to connect the dots in our life's story. It is an opportunity to transcend limiting beliefs and evolve beyond fear.

What happens is that the sensation of Knowing grabs your attention and places it on the next move or on the immediate decision to be made. Knowing, with the sensation of foreboding, puts you in a state of high alert and keen awareness; what you know resonates deeply within and is accompanied by high energy. Although our ego (our belief system) will be resistant to the sensation of foreboding or to what it perceives is wrong or frightening, the high energy and alertness override the ego and motivate action. The strong resonance of Knowing shows up without the intellectual reasoning of the mind. It shows us that we are connected to a divine intelligence, a spiritual energy—whatever name you have for it—and in this, there is no fear.

If you have experiences of Knowing accompanied by a strong feeling of foreboding or warning, notice it and take whatever action is required. Later, go in for a deeper look and see if you can locate the message of peace and rightness that accompanied the foreboding.

~~~~~~~~~~~~~~~~~~~

Seventeen years ago, I went to Oklahoma to pick up my mother and bring her back to Texas to spend the week with me. Both parents were retired; Dad was seventy, and Mother was in her late sixties. Mother had planned the visit a few weeks earlier, and she was looking forward to spending the week with my four-year-old son. Dad was to stay behind and tend to the cattle.

Just as Mother and I were packing the car to return to Texas, I said to her, "I don't have a good feeling about you coming with me." Mother seemed relieved and acknowledged that she was feeling the same way. So she stayed behind. I returned to Texas that Saturday night. The following Monday evening, I received a distressing call from my sister saying that Dad had been admitted into the hospital and was in critical condition. In a matter of hours, he was flown by helicopter to a Dallas hospital. The following three weeks were up and down.

The doctors were doing everything they could to stabilize my father enough to have open heart surgery. Mother told the family that Dad would never return home. We kept telling her to think positive. Three weeks later, the day following his surgery, Dad passed to the other side. He lived for three weeks, giving us all time to process the inevitable.

A few weeks after things had settled down, Mother confided to me that she wasn't being negative when she said that Dad wasn't going to make it; she knew that Dad wouldn't ever go home with her again.

I know that I was being prepared. I was dating a doctor at the time. Knowing my father's condition, he told me to accept reality; my dad (outside of a miracle) wasn't going to make it. I still didn't want to accept what he was saying. Yet at the same time, something interesting happened. One day, while in the kitchen thinking about my father, I heard a noise of something hitting the kitchen floor.

I looked down to find my heart-shaped ceramic magnet that had hung on my refrigerator door for a couple of years. It was a strong magnet and to remove it actually took a little effort. It had fallen off the door all by itself, landing at my feet, and was broken in half. I picked it up and glued it back together with super glue. It wouldn't glue back together. I attempted different glue. That one didn't stick it together, either. Third try, third glue. Still, it would not adhere.

It was at that moment I knew that dad would never return from the hospital. His heart was irreparable. It was now time for me to accept that reality. What other choice did I have? I could resist reality and suffer or I could accept it, learn what I needed to learn, and move on. Either way, the reality was the same.

- -

FINDING YOUR WHISPER MOMENTS
Locate Your Experience of Knowing

Remember a time when *you knew that you knew.* Later, you shouted, "I knew it! I told you so!" What did you know? This isn't when you had a strong belief about something. With Knowing, you had no clue how or why you knew. Go into the feeling of Knowing and feel the sureness of it. **Write your experience of Knowing.**

Now find a time when you believed something very strongly; you really thought you knew something, and you later found out you were wrong. Describe the differences between these feelings of strong belief and Knowing. Get comfortable with how each of these feels within you. You are learning to recognize the distinct differences between the sensations of your Whisper and the sensations of your beliefs. **Write your experience here:**

I had been divorced for five years. My children were grown, and the idea came to me to move back to Japan. I had lived and gone to school there as a teenager and had recently been back for a school reunion. Seeing myself living in Japan was a Knowing, but I had not a clue as to the how! As things began to magically unfold, I realized that I just had to allow things to show up. And they did!

Information would come to me from nowhere, and I soon discovered that I just had to get out of the way. I was able to transfer the deed of my townhouse back to the original owner after someone shared this idea with me. An offer to teach English in a Japanese girls' high school came from the headmaster, who I had known since I was thirteen! A former classmate helped me find an apartment to live in. I happened upon many of my furnishings during the monthly big trash days. What I now know from this is that when I Know, there is no doubt, only certainty, and the details take care of themselves. I know to trust the Knowing.

Mary Helen Kuehner, Round Rock, TX

CHAPTER 7

The Sixth Distinct Experience

❖ Inspiration ❖

The Energy of Creation

Inspiration is the experience of creative arousal and spontaneous movement toward fulfilling an idea that stimulates you with joy. This spontaneous and inspired thought or idea has the feel of a guess to it, an intuitive hit, but with a deep sense of accuracy. It is a download of such immense energy that you have to move; you have to flow with that energy. With Inspiration, there is no procrastination.

High and light, the energy is so compelling; you are filled with desire to do what you are inspired to, and you can't wait to get started. Curious excitement washes over you. You begin to notice the information related to your Inspiration all around you, and you see things you didn't see before. When you act on Inspiration, the universe supports you, its doors fling open, and obstacles melt away.

Your Inspiration inspires others. A key distinction of Inspiration emanating from your Whisper is that it serves and benefits others. It is a creation of something that inspires others and lifts them in transformative ways. Inspired works of art, music, writing, and architecture are examples of this. Inspired community projects, organizations, and schools are often created from the high level of energy that comes with Inspiration.

You may, however, be inspired to cook a wonderful meal for only one person. You may be inspired to write a story for your child or do the costuming for a theatre production. You may be inspired to take up knitting or to build a house. Inspiration serves and touches others in many ways. Your painting does not have to hang in the Metropolitan Museum of Art to be considered inspirational. A guest visiting your home who looks at your painting may be inspired to do something creative as well. A guest eating an inspired meal may ask for the recipe and serve it to others or simply be filled with well-being and delight.

Sometimes, when we receive Inspiration (in spirit), we may not act on it; we think what we are feeling isn't important or deserving of our time and effort. You may experience some doubt with Inspiration if you have a belief that you cannot create something that doesn't already exist. You may feel silly that you have a strong desire to do something you have never done before or are unskilled at or lack experience in.

For this reason, it is critical to understand that because of these beliefs, Inspiration is the distinct experience of guidance often ignored; and when ignored, it is the one that affects us the hardest. If not acted upon, we may feel an immediate lack of energy. The tremendous surge of liveliness and sensation of energy and desire that accompany Inspiration dissipate and scatter, and may lodge in the body. Not acting on the heightened energy that accompanies Inspiration may feel like depression, guilt, fatigue, and lethargy. This is discussed later, with greater detail, in Chapter 11, Beliefs That Block Trust – Uncovering the Symptoms of Resistance.

It helps to know that Inspiration is your Whisper telling you that *you can* create this! Move with the energy, follow the idea, take it one step at a time, and allow your inner guidance to bring to you the people and the knowledge that will fulfill the inspired, creative idea.

FINDING YOUR WHISPER MOMENTS

Locate the Energy of Inspiration

Find a time when you were completely and utterly inspired to action. You couldn't wait to get started; you may have had doubts, but you acted on the inspiration anyway.

Can you find it? Write out your story and include the idea that came to you. What did the energy feel like? Be specific; locating these qualities shows you how you receive these sensations.

Write your story here:

Now find a time when you were inspired to do something but you didn't do it. Perhaps you were inspired to paint or draw, and you went out and got all the supplies, but you didn't follow through. Look around; what do you have unfinished that *originated* as Inspiration? What happened to the energy? How did it feel?

Write what happened when you didn't follow the energy of Inspiration:

Like all children, I longed for acceptance and validation from those around me in my formative years. As I grew up, I longed to hear "Good job. You are special. I am so proud of you." I never heard any of those words from my parents. The lack of positive feedback set the stage for virtually a lifetime of me being consumed with self-doubt and low self-esteem, which had me settle for less in my relationships with others.

As a young woman, I became involved with men who also did not speak kind words to me, whose strict control aggressively chipped away at my very soul to the point that I barely knew who I was by the time my autumn years were on the horizon.

On February 6th, 2006, my mother went into the hospital for a simple operation. We thought she would be home in a week, but it turned into months. During the first three weeks, I sat and watched my mother lay helpless in the ICU. As I watched her, I wondered if she had done what she wanted to do with her life and if she had any regrets.

Surprisingly, I also came to realize that the very questions I had for my mother were my own. I hadn't realized my own desires, and I didn't know my true passion. I had been so busy living for the comfort and pleasure of everyone else that I had not truly lived for myself.

It was during this time that God showed me the light. He put in my heart that it was now my time to shine—my time to give to others, to make a difference, and to change lives. In the Methodist hospital's waiting room, I immediately started sketching, planning, and redirecting my life's journey; and it was in that very room that Women Power Talk Radio was born.

The show's purpose was, and still is, to inspire, empower, and uplift women like myself: boomer women who had settled or given up on their dreams but who wanted to dream again. The very thought of such a thing invigorated and inspired me to the very core and filled me with complete joy.

Nevertheless, there was still one major obstacle to overcome: I was neither an author nor a speaker. Except for twenty-five years of phone sales, I had no real expertise—or so I thought. Refusing to give up on my dream, I signed up for a course offered by my mentor, Alex Mandossian. With his course, I discovered that I could become an expert by interviewing experts, coaches, gurus, and bestselling authors. And that is exactly what I did. I started interviewing boomer women willing to share their inspiring stories and messages.

I have been producing my show for the past twenty-one months. I now have listeners all across the United States, Canada,

Australia, South Africa, Europe, and Asia. I've received letters from countless women who shared how the interviews made a difference in their lives. I can't even begin to tell you what a wonderful feeling and journey this has been. Not only have I been able to create and produce a show that empowers women, but through it all, some of my own dreams have come true.

Raven Blair Davis, Houston, TX

SECTION TWO

Trusting Your Essential Whisper

CHAPTER 8

❧ A Template for Trust ❧

Creating the Experience of Trust

This section is about trusting inner guidance with absolute certainty. You've come to the part where you develop awareness and take deliberate, conscious action to trust and follow the whispers of your soul, which really are the whispers of your heart.

Trusting with absolute certainty—is that even possible? Recognizing your Whisper in the previous section was pretty easy because you simply had to go back to your experiences and pull up memories. You remembered (brought back to awareness) events and situations of the Six Distinct Ways guidance moved you to manifest something or answer an essential question or wondering you had. Within each of those occurrences sat the sensations of the Whisper—the discernable signature of its voice. And perhaps you discovered how you've followed guidance without realizing that was what you were doing.

You may have remembered some experiences, but not all of them. Even without specific memories of all six distinct ways, recognizing them as they show up will still be easy because of the *memory you created* when you read the descriptions of each one. For example, if you were told to pick someone up at the airport who you hadn't met before, but you had a picture of that person, would you recognize him as he approached you? Of course you would. You'd have a picture of what this person looked like, and as he approached, you would match his face to the picture.

As you read these words, the imagination makes pictures in your mind of the words and their meaning. These images give you a template; they create a memory of an experience. As you look at the picture of the person you are waiting for at the airport, you imagine meeting him. Even though you've never met, the imagination produces an experience in your mind, a template. Likewise, even if you couldn't recall a direct memory of Collapsed Time when you read the description, you still formed a picture of it, so that when the sensations and experience of Collapsed Time actually occur, you'll recognize it.

Just becoming familiar with the six distinct ways and the sensations will give you a pattern for the memory. So don't be concerned if you haven't been able to recognize all six ways yet; you will.

Manifesting Certainty

So let's go back to trust and how all of this relates to trusting your Essential Whisper.

This chapter started off with a question: Trusting with absolute certainty—is that even possible? Yes! But first, you must understand trust as an *inner thing*, not an outer thing.

Sometimes, we look outside ourselves for something or someone to give us trust. We say, "You must do this before I can trust you," or "I will trust my Whisper when it does this for me." Many have stated that they can sometimes recognize inner guidance, but they don't always trust it. You can't find trust out there. Even trusting the sun to rise in the morning has nothing to do with the sun.

So let's begin by getting clear on what trust is. What is something you trust? Go ahead; take a few moments to answer that question. Got something? Perhaps you trust the sun will rise in the morning, or you trust the mail will get delivered tomorrow. When you have it, then answer this: What prompts (motivates) you to trust this? If you trust the sun to rise in the morning, maybe you would answer, "It's because it has risen every morning of my life." Again, take a few moments to think about this. What does trust feel like in your body?

Trust has a feeling of certainty to it; after all, if you feel uncertain about something, you don't trust it, right? The feeling of certainty comes from perceiving the evidence or experience of something. You have proof and confidence that what you trust is reliable and dependable. If you trust the sun to rise, then no doubt you have racked up days, months, years of experience that the sun appears each morning, so you have complete trust in this. Certainty is the absence of doubt. To be without doubt is to have single-minded trust. You have verification. This is the difference between trust and faith. Faith requires you to have certainty in something that you are unable to prove for yourself.

Although trust and faith are synonymous, faith requires you to know or believe something without evidence. It is difficult to tell someone to have faith, because within faith is a seed of doubt. Faith requires that you use willpower to deny the feeling of doubt you have. How often have you tried to have faith in something only to fall short of having *complete* faith? Thoughts of doubt inevitably show up, because in order to feel certainty, we require evidence, and there isn't any in simple faith. You are not required to have faith in order to recognize, trust, and follow inner guidance with absolute certainty.

So where does the evidence of inner guidance, the sensations we feel, come from? Here's where it gets interesting. You manifest it. That's right; you create certainty by perceiving the evidence you require. You see, to manifest anything is to make it evident, which means the object or the experience is readily perceived by your senses and easily understood or recognized by the mind. Evidence is nothing more than perceptual manifestation. In other words, what we see, we've created—we've made manifest.

Try this: look at something in front of you; select just one object. It may be a book, a glass, a pencil, or a toaster. Are you certain it's there? This is not a trick question. If you see it, you are probably certain that it is there. As you look at something, you have visual evidence it is there; you perceive its existence and trust what you perceive. Now ask yourself, "How did that get there?"

When we did this in our Inner Advantage Training[1] class, each participant was led through an exercise to look at each object in front of him and realize he manifested every single one. This is powerful! It is powerful to realize you are the creator of your world, the one who gives you your experiences of what you see and of what you sense. Remember, to manifest is to make something perceptually evident. You manifested what is in front of you.

Understanding trust is about knowing how you manifest certainty in your life, because it is you who manifests the evidence and has the direct experience of what you are trusting. The Six Distinct Experiences are your evidence of the inner sensations of guidance. You can trust them, because you are the one who perceives and has evidence of them. It is you doing the trusting here; it is you who is manifesting the trust. As you readily perceive the sensations of your essential guidance, they become clear, apparent, distinct, certain, evident, obvious, palpable, materialized, and unambiguous.

Trust is belief in the truth of something and confidence in the reliability of a thing or person. So it may have been scary following inner guidance up until now, because it meant taking action on the guidance only if you were confident taking that action without fear or disappointment. Nonsense!

Whenever we believe that we must have trust and blind faith first, before we can follow inner guidance, then we have to conjure up willpower to develop that trust, certainty, and confidence. That's backwards. Trust, as we have discovered, is manifested as evidence you perceive. Simply perceiving evidence—having the experience of something—is enough to create trust. You can have absolute certainty because the evidence, the experience, and the sensations of inner guidance sit right inside you.

Trust is a State of Mind

Furthermore, trust has nothing to do with what is true. Consider this: Do you know someone who trusts her lover or a friend, and you can't figure out why she does? You perceive the person trusted to be, well, untrustworthy, and you have lots of evidence for it, too! Do you trust something or someone that others tell you not to trust?

The act of trust is a state of mind. It is a *belief* in the truth and reliability of something or someone. And herein lies the dilemma.

Belief in what we think is true does not make what is believed inherently true. But it will feel true and certain to us.

Our actions spring from what we believe; we respond to and act out our beliefs. For centuries, people would not embark on ocean voyages for fear of falling off the earth. The belief was that the earth was flat. The earth was considered the center of the universe. The belief was that the sun spun around the earth. Now we've discovered galaxies so vast as to be unimaginable—well, almost. *Star Trek*, the popular television space adventure, has shown what the imagination is capable of creating.

You believe what you believe, and not only would it be hopeless to tell you to change your beliefs, you couldn't anyway—until you sat with a belief, looked it squarely in the eye, and determined if it was *really* true. The fact is, people will fight to the death and kill others to defend what they believe is true. Galileo Galilei, astronomer and physicist, escaped being put to death—unlike his predecessor Giordano Bruno—for his heliocentric theories (the belief that sun is the center of our solar system). But he was eventually forced to recant his theories, which contradicted the beliefs of the church, and ultimately spent the last years of his life under house arrest. Bruno had been prosecuted in Rome and burned at the stake as a heretic. History is littered with battles of beliefs, and in truth, all war is the defense of some strongly held belief.

You can know what is inherently true because truth resides within your heart and feels peaceful. Truth is neutral; it is its own nature regardless of our belief in it. Truth is timeless; it doesn't waver or fluctuate across the centuries and millennium. Truth is known; we are wired to know the truth.[2] Do you recognize these feelings? They are the inner sensations of guidance; peacefulness, neutrality, timelessness, certainty. **Inner guidance whispers the truth to you.** When you move away from truth (ignore or resist inner guidance) you will feel discomfort. *When you move away from truth it's because you believe something to be true that isn't, and the sensations of guidance will alert you and set off an alarm of discomfort in your body.* You can count on it. These sensations are what you can trust. That's good news because …

There Is a Skeptic in Our Midst

Have you noticed that the feeling of truthfulness isn't listed as a sensation of the Whisper (peacefulness, joy, spaciousness, openness, neutrality, presence, energy, sureness, resonance, alignment)?

What we feel as true is not the same as truth, which is neutral, complete, and matches reality—what is. Consider the following:

- All beliefs are true and feel true to the believer
- All thoughts believed will feel true

Go ahead and test this out for yourself. Take any belief you have and see if it feels true to you. There probably isn't any surprise here; after all, that is the nature of belief. Belief is any premise you hold as true, whether knowingly (consciously) or unknowingly (unconsciously). In fact, most of your beliefs are unknown to you and reside below your level of awareness.

Remember the story of how La Rue honestly filled out the true-or-false questionnaire only to discover she got nine out of ten wrong? We have beliefs we don't even consciously know about, and this is how we make ourselves wrong and sabotage our most cherished dreams. We rely on the feeling of truth, but the feeling of truth is tied to our beliefs. **The closest sensation we can rely on for truth is neutrality.** It's non-attachment to what is. Truth has no agenda, no desire for any particular outcome. Belief does! War is what happens when we defend our beliefs, and that is a pretty strong agenda.

All of your beliefs make up your *belief system*. This is just a fancy way of saying your beliefs make up your worldview, the way you see and perceive the world around you and, ultimately, how you act and behave in it. It is the *you* you call *I*. I am _____. I must_____. I can _____. I should

_____. I can't _____. The skeptic is the part of you that doesn't believe or accept anything new or outside of your worldview.

What this means is your mind (belief system, ego) will determine the compatibility of any new information, beliefs, and ideas to the existing information, beliefs, and ideas you hold. So, regardless of whether a particular belief is helpful to you or not, it gets in only if it is compatible with your existing ideas of the world. That is what it means to be skeptical; it's the mind's way of looking for compatibility.

While reading the last paragraph, for example, you were interpreting what you read through your belief system. You took in the words and transcribed them through the filters of your experience, ideas, and perception. What is written on this page will be interpreted differently by everyone who reads it. No matter how clearly or succinctly or accurately these words are selected, you come to this page, to this book, as an individualized expression of being with a unique viewpoint.

So when it comes to developing trust, be aware that it can't be dependent on the feeling of truthfulness. When you experience an Urge, for example, with intense energy and desire to go to the store, yet you have nothing in mind to purchase, watch out! The skeptic will jump in and tell you that going to the store for *no reason* is incompatible to a belief you might hold about wasting time or money, or not having time or money. Yet, as you have already discovered, when you follow an Urge, the reason becomes apparent, although perhaps later.

One Action One Decision

Trusting something requires a level of reliability, which comes from proof. We need evidence and proof that our trust is deserved. The sensations of guidance act as that proof through the Six Distinct Experiences. As you readily and continually perceive the sensations of the Whisper, they become clear and apparent to you.

There is one action and one decision that will make it really easy to continually perceive the sensations of the Whisper. The one action is the action of acknowledgment. The one decision is the decision to open your awareness. These act as inner commitments to live your life in partnership with your Whisper. Read on to learn how these two ways to develop trust will propel you into the world of the Whisper, with certainty.

CHAPTER 9

❧ One Action to Take ❧

Five Simple Acknowledgments

The one action that shifts your perception and manifests trust is to acknowledge the Whisper. That doesn't sound like much of an action, does it? Yet it is. It's a movement of attitude; it's an action that shifts and opens perception.

Don't take the act of acknowledgment lightly, however. This one action is a critical component of trust. Without acknowledgment, it is very hard to follow or act on the sensations of guidance, because, very simply, you won't even recognize it when it occurs. Acknowledgment allows you to see and hear the Whisper and gives you evidence that creates certainty.

In one version of the myth of King Arthur and the Knights of the Round Table, Merlin, the notable wizard who advised the king and who represented the new way of an emerging Christianity, faced an adversary named Queen Mab. Queen Mab ruled the fairies and was the embodiment of the old way, the way of magic. She was a formidable foe as her magic was very powerful. Merlin's magic was no match for her incredible powers. Yet, in the end, she was defeated. How? Merlin advised the people in the countryside to ignore her. They stopped acknowledging her presence and her power. She faded away and was forgotten.

This speaks to the magnitude of acknowledgement. Think of it this way: if there was a knock on the door from a most welcomed visitor, but you couldn't hear the knock, what would happen? The visitor would stand outside, waiting to be let in, and you wouldn't even know it. To acknowledge is to have knowledge of, and knowledge is what you've given yourself by reading this book—knowledge of the distinct experiences and sensations of the Whisper. It's the knock on the door. But hearing the knock isn't enough. To acknowledge also means to accept. To enjoy your special guest, sit, and sip tea, you have to open the door and invite your visitor in. You have to trust the knock as a call to action. You've got to walk over, turn the knob, and open the door. Action fortifies trust. Trust fortifies certainty.

Acknowledgement is the one-action step. The five simple ways of acknowledgment listed below help you to trust guidance so you can recognize it, accept it, and act on it. Take a look at the definition below pulled right out of the dictionary:[1]

Acknowledge: to recognize the rights, authority or status of; to disclose knowledge or agreement with; to make known the receipt of; to recognize as genuine or valid; to express gratitude or obligation.

Acknowledgement is the *intentional and deliberate action* of trusting the existence of an internal wisdom and an abiding love. It is the only action you need to take; the rest follows naturally. Isn't that good to know? Below, each of the pieces of acknowledgment is defined in a bit more detail.

The First Way to Acknowledgement: *Recognize the Essential Voice Within as Authority*

The word *authority* can ruffle a few feathers, so it is diligent to clarify the meaning—after all, do you trust authority all the time? The government? The police? Your boss? Since we are talking about trusting with absolute certainty, it is essential that *what* you trust is indeed something you can trust, something you consider reliable and true. An authority is someone or something that has influence and power. So what power are we to trust?

Are you ready? Read this next sentence carefully, because this is what you are going to give authority to; this is what you are going to acknowledge as the highest expression of power.

The Essential Whisper arises from love, so what you are acknowledging is *love*. The Whisper is your individualized expression of the complete source of love. The sensations of what we are referring to as the Whisper emanate from love. Peacefulness, neutrality, energy, presence, timelessness, and the sensation of expansiveness are all individualized aspects of love. Love is beyond definition; defining it singularizes it, compartmentalizes it. The sensations shift our perception of what is, in any moment, so we can see the beauty of it all. This is to know love.

You may have noticed that love is not listed as a sensation. Love is not a sensation of inner guidance; it's the source of inner guidance. It is what it is and is therefore the authority. What we feel as love is an emotion of physical love, of one body toward another body. This *feeling* of emotional and conditional love is not what we are speaking of here.

Love cannot be defined as a singular object or state of being. It is simply all of it, and to delineate it and classify love is to pull it out and separate it from *all that is*. By acknowledging the authority of love, you are giving yourself evidence of love. When you open the door to the Whisper, you are opening your heart to love.

The Second Way to Acknowledgement: *Know Inner Guidance Can and Does Speak to You*

By this time, you have found several experiences in the past when inner guidance has prompted you. And even if you haven't found them all, remember, you learned that you've created an experience of them in your memory anyway, and you'll recognize the sensations as they occur. Begin to notice when these sensations show up day to day, moment to moment, going forward. This is living in the presence of the Whisper. The second way to acknowledgement is to become present with the Whisper and continuously notice the sensations of guidance. After all, if the Whisper is continuously speaking to you, then you have the opportunity to continuously receive it.

The Third Way to Acknowledgement: *Receive the Messages and Guidance*

It's noted above, in the second way, that you are continuously spoken to and you have the opportunity to continuously receive guidance. The act of receiving, however, is not passive; it requires that you take and accept what is given. If you lay a gift before me, you have given it to me, right? What if I don't accept it, and the gift lays there unopened? Have I received it? If I pick it up, open it, and say, "Thank you," feeling full gratitude for the gift, then I have fully received it. The Whisper speaks continuously, yet it is only when it is actively received that the gift becomes yours and the Whisper is acknowledged.

The Fourth Way to Acknowledgement: Recognize the Whisper as Valid and Genuine

You have received and felt the sensations of inner guidance many times, even though you may not have known that's what they were. You probably recalled several instances of this in the Finding Your Whisper Moments exercises sprinkled throughout Section One. Take a moment and think of one now. Got one? As you recall your experience of following guidance and how it all turned out, ask yourself this: "Was it valid?"

Validity is subjective. Something cannot stand on its own as valid. It has to be considered valid. Your experiences are what convince you of the validity of the Whisper. The heading above says *Recognize the Whisper as Valid and Genuine*. Notice is doesn't say the Whisper *is* valid and genuine. If it isn't considered valid to you then you couldn't be convinced or persuaded that it was, right? When you locate these events and notice how your life was always guided and has unfolded perfectly, you will readily come to know in your heart that what you receive is authentic, genuine, and valid. On the other hand, if you do not acknowledge the Whisper as valid, it is unlikely you will ever trust its messages.

The Fifth Way to Acknowledgement: *Express Gratitude.*

The state of gratitude immediately shifts perception. A troubled, doubtful mind will come to rest in a heart open to gratitude. To get there, a simple thank you will do nicely.

Throughout the years, people would tell me, "If only I knew how to talk to guidance, my life would be easier." Often, they were shown exactly how guidance did talk to them, but they didn't listen. Well, early on, I wasn't any different.

Shortly after the experience of hearing my soul's voice in Dr. Demartini's class, I considered moving. I had some financial goals I wanted to achieve before I moved, so I planned the move for the end of the year, several months away.

One morning, my inner voice screamed at me. Internally, it yelled, "You'll be moving sooner than you think!" Shaking and wide awake, I thought, When? Where? In my mind's eye, I saw an image of a place in Las Colinas, a city outside of Dallas. "Go there." I didn't go. I wasn't very good at obeying yet.

The next morning, I was awakened again. "Go there, today!"

This time, after I left work, I drove over to a gated community. I said to the man at the gate, "Can I go in and drive around?"

"Oh no, ma'am. I can't let you in."

"Are there any places for lease?"

"Here's a list of realtors. Give them a call."

One name popped out on the list of about twenty. She came immediately. The place she showed me was exactly what I imagined, except it was considerably more than I wanted to pay. My soul said, "Sign the contract." Yes, it did. I heard it. Trembling, I signed the contract for several thousand dollars. For days, I experienced major anxiety, but, contractually committed, I began buying furniture and getting ready. Just a few weeks prior to my move, the realtor told me the owner had changed his mind and wanted to move back into his place. I said, "Of course he can!" I felt relief wash over me, but that's not the amazing part. He refunded the deposit, plus three thousand six hundred dollars for the inconvenience. I made thirty six hundred dollars by signing that contract! That was the easiest money I've ever made. I ended up in a house that was brand-new, never lived in, on a lake, and I had a pocket full of cash!

My soul's voice never screamed at me again. It never had to. You see, I wasn't accustomed to paying attention. I was sleeping most of the time—not literally, of course, but I simply didn't know how to intentionally pay attention. My inner voice screamed at me to wake me up, until I finally acknowledged it and followed its guidance. For years and years, I prayed, "Give me faith; give me faith." Then one day, I had a revelation—faith strengthens with action. I acted on urges or inspiration even while shaking in my boots sometimes. I acted, and it always worked out. In fact, I can't remember a time when it didn't work out. I can remember dozens of times, however, when following my plan didn't pan out. Eventually, I came to see that the soul is fluid and unlimited and could be trusted.

CHAPTER 10

❧ The One Decision to Make ❧

Four Channels to Awareness

The action of *acknowledgement* offers you a way to gain credibility toward the Whisper and your experiences of this guidance. You can call these experiences flukes, accidents, strokes of luck, or mere coincidences. Or you can trust yourself to be the designer of a divine partnership with the essence of your being and the creator of your experiences. Either way, you always have a choice.

The problem is, you may not be awake to your choices. Remember the *skeptic*, the voice of your belief system? Well, if your guidance is communicating something to you that doesn't get by the skeptic (isn't compatible to your belief system), you may not even be able to hear or discern the Whisper's subtle voice. The second step for developing trust is to open your awareness and insight. Open awareness allows you to readily perceive the Whisper as it continually speaks to you. Perception, sensitivity, and experiences of inner guidance are what give you proof and strengthen trust.

Have you noticed that the Six Distinct Ways automatically override the belief system, at least initially? In each of the six ways, a state of presence fills you, and in that moment, beliefs are suspended. When you feel Urge, it fills you with a sudden and intense energy to act. No amount of reasoning can change the sensations enveloping you. When Inspiration strikes, you are energized to create and manifest something in your life. When Knowing surges through your cells, there's not one molecule of doubt allowed, and your beliefs are vanquished.

Inspiration may stimulate and enthuse you to work on an idea, but if you begin believing that you can't do it or you won't have time because you've never done anything like this before, then the energy of Inspiration will eventually dissipate, leaving you drained and disappointed.

Quiet the skeptic's voice (the voices in your head) with the decision to expand your awareness. There are four channels to open awareness, four ways to consciously tune in to the palpable sensations within. Choose the channel(s) that resonate with you; any one of them will expand your awareness, making it easier to recognize and trust your guidance.

The First Channel to Open Awareness: Conscious Choice

It may sound silly to have to make a *conscious choice*. Did you know you have over sixty thousand thoughts a day? Which ones do you remember today? Which ones did you act on? Which ones tripped you up and caused a cycle of stress, anxiety, or frustration? Did you hear inner guidance today? It continuously whispers to you; did you hear it?

Every moment of every day, we are doing one of two things: we are following inner guidance or not. Something as simple as an Urge to go to the bathroom can get ignored by the voice in your head that tells you to go after the commercial.

On the other hand, when you *decide* to follow the wisdom of your soul, that becomes the *only* decision you have to make. By doing so, you now have access to all the options available beyond your belief system. *Making just that one choice to follow your Whisper opens you up to unlimited choices,* and they are brought to you as Urges, Wonderment, Inspiration, and Knowing, as well as the myriad ways the Whisper interacts and communicates specific messages to you (see Chapter 14). Your day unfolds by simply following the energy of what you are directed to do, each next step.

Making a statement of what you'd like to consciously choose works rather nicely.

You might say, "Today I decide to be aware of my inner voice, which speaks to me through the inner sensations of openness, peace, spaciousness, presence, and energy."

You will find that listening to your inner voice is actually easier than trying to figure things out yourself. You have ease of movement in your life. Your actions flow from inner sensations, and everything that needs to get done gets done. Often, we make decisions believing we have no choice. *"I had to make that decision! I had no choice."* It *does* feel like there's no choice when it is unconsciously and automatically carried out by the belief system. When a conscious selection or a choice is not made, then the habitual pattern of your mind, directed by your belief system and those sixty thousand recycled thoughts, continues to be activated.

By simply making the conscious decision to tune in within for the sensations of inner guidance, you have taken leaps to wake yourself up. Ultimately, you are deciding what experiences you'd like to have and create in your life.

The Second Channel to Open Awareness: Focused Attention

We are always guided and constantly spoken to, but we often miss the Whisper because our attention is not on receiving its information. Instead, our attention is distracted and pulled by the thoughts and chatter going on in our mind.

Many people do not know how to *deliberately direct* their attention, and therefore may become easily distracted and scattered.

Here is a very simple exercise that helps you to place your attention on what you want to focus on.

Sit quietly for a few moments. Where are you? Look around. What do you see? Are there other people there with you? Are you alone? Is there a pet nearby?

Are you indoors? Outdoors?

What is the temperature?

What sounds do you hear?

What odors do you smell?

What is your state of mind? Relaxed? Tense?

Look directly at your knee.

Very good. Now turn your head to the right and look at what is there. If you are indoors, is it a wall, a window, a door? Really look at what you see.

Now turn your head to the left and look at what is there. Really look at what you see.

Very good.

(The following is done with eyes closed, so read first, then do the exercise.)

Close your eyes and put your attention on your knee for a moment.

Without moving your head, move your attention to the right.

Without moving your head, move your attention to the left.

Open your eyes.

Excellent. This is a brief exercise in placing attention where you direct it.

Attention can be directed deliberately and intentionally. Did you notice that when you placed your attention, with closed eyes, on your knee, you could feel your knee and see it in your mind's eye? How about when you placed your attention to the right and then to the left?

At first, attention is like an untamed horse running wild. When it is trained, it will go where you consciously place it. With practice, you can control the reins of your attention.

The Third Channel to Open Awareness: Focused Intention

Intention is establishing *what* we want to pay attention to. Intention sets the parameter for what we create in our life. Intentions guide creation. Placing your intention on how you want to respond to the Whisper is how you manifest (create) your experiences of the Whisper. Deliberate intention deliberately creates. In this case, what you are creating is evidence of the Whisper. You are creating trust, and the evidence of your experiences will give you certainty.

Intentions are clearest when they align with what you sincerely desire to create in your life. As you set your intention to align and partner with your soul and place your attention on being guided from there, this becomes the truest, clearest intention you can set.

The Fourth Channel to Open Awareness: Noticing

Noticing is how you observe and interact with the world around you. Noticing is taking in, detecting, and observing what is occurring from moment to moment. There is no judgment or interpretation when you notice. It is you being aware of what is, with no criticism or analysis about what is happening.

Noticing is watching.

A friend noticed that, through her despondency after the death of her mother, she had thoughts that would interrupt her pain. "What's for dinner?" "I should take out the dog." Even through the grief, she noticed thoughts would just appear, and the grief would switch to thoughts of dinner, then to the dog. Eventually, the grief lessened, as staying present filled her day with more and more joy.

That's what noticing does. You study yourself. Noticing keeps you in the present. You can't notice the past or notice the future. To notice is to see what you see right now. As you read this, notice your breath. Were you able to switch from reading this page to noticing your breath? What or who did the switching? What is doing the breathing? Did you notice that the observer is not you, the breather? The observer is the part of you noticing the breathing. In order to notice anything, your mind has to become still—even if there is a lot of activity going on around you, even if you are in the middle of an argument. In order to notice, you tune in and access a place in you that is still, watchful, and neutral.

From the perspective of the observer within, you become aware of your thoughts and of the various ways that you respond and react in your life. Noticing opens the way to simple awareness. You can tell yourself to notice instead of judge. With noticing, you become aware, and you do so without activating judgment.

These four channels to open awareness allow increased consciousness and responsiveness, and they are simple ways to heighten your perception of intuitive sensations. The decision to open your awareness increases your ability to trust the Six Distinct Ways of Snap-Click, Collapsed Time and Space, Urge, Wonderment, Knowing, and Inspiration. Opening your awareness is how you pay attention to these experiences so that you can recognize them when they show up.

Acknowledgement and awareness are the two easy ways to step into trusting your essential self. Now that you trust the sensations of guidance, it's time to expose the symptoms of resistance and the beliefs that will creep in from time to time and keep you from trusting guidance.

CHAPTER 11

❧ The Beliefs that Block Trust ❧

Uncovering the Symptoms of Resistance

In the previous chapters, you learned that anything you believe will feel true and be known to you as true. And you may remember that most of what you believe is in your subconscious and that you aren't even aware of all the beliefs you have. Yet, unquestionably, all beliefs feel true. That's because *all beliefs are formed emotionally*; they are based on the *perceived evidence* we have for the belief.

Is it any wonder that hearing inner guidance has been a bit confusing? You might be asking, "If the thoughts in my head feel true, then how can I know what is really true?" Good question! And it's a question that so many people ask. In fact, over the years, these are some of the questions clients have asked again and again:

- How can I know when my inner voice is talking to me?
- How do I know what to do?
- How do I know if what I am doing is the right thing to do?
- How do I separate out God's voice, or truth, from my regular thoughts and the other internal voices?

It is not suggested you attempt to drop your beliefs or try to look at them all. It's not necessary to do that to discern the Whisper. Fortunately, there is one language we all speak: the language of feeling. Our stories may differ, even our beliefs may differ, but the language of feeling is the same for all of us. That's why you are repeatedly reminded to always *bring yourself back to the sensations of the Whisper.*

Here's why …

It's not that we don't want to know the truth, but rather, that we are not aware of what the truth is. The thinking mind can only know about something.

That was what David Hawkins, PhD found after over twenty years of research, detailed in his book, *Power vs. Force*. Dr. Hawkins explains:

> There is only one identical question underlying all human problems … and that is what truth is and by what means is it knowable … Humility is a critical quality because it is based on the recognition and incorporation of the basic truth that, unaided, the human mind is intrinsically incapable of discovering truth.[1]

This is verified in Evo-K sessions, as well. In Evolutional Kinesiology, clients are shown, through muscle response feedback, the beliefs that get in the way of what they want to create in their lives. This technology enables the Evo-K facilitator to bypass the conscious self and access the unconscious cellular memories. Often, the client is surprised that a certain belief he installed, perhaps as a child, is still operating in his belief system.

This is a powerful yet gentle way to make what is subconscious, conscious. Very often, it is helpful to have a qualified facilitator or practitioner to work with when continued self-sabotage occurs; after all, many beliefs are transparent and unseen by us. Yet the questions guiding this book and listed above can be answered by incorporating the one action and the one decision outlined in the previous chapter. They are: 1) acknowledge the sensations of inner guidance; and 2) open your awareness to these sensations.

So once again, you cannot use "it feels true to me" as a gauge for trust. This is really important to understand. *You've already given yourself evidence for every belief you hold,* so every single one feels true to you. Let's say you have an Urge to move to another city. The sensations you feel are intense energy, along with a strong desire to move, a feeling of openness, and an internal lightness. Everywhere you look, you see moving vans. You receive real estate notices in the mail. You even have dreams about moving. You feel inspired to research the bank interest rates and check out the job market in other cities. Yet something keeps you from acting on these sensations. What is it?

It is beliefs that you hold. You don't believe you will find a job. Maybe you've moved before, and it was a real hassle. You don't believe you have the money to move. You don't have time to look for work. You'll wait for the interest rates to fall, the housing prices to drop, the workload on your job to lighten. It would be better to move after the winter. It would be better to move after you get your tax refund. There's no limit to the beliefs someone could have that could contradict the sensations received from the Whisper. The sensations were clear, but if your beliefs don't support them, you won't trust and act on the Whisper; you will resist or ignore it, because all your reasons feel true.

Face it. Every single belief will feel true and right. It makes sense—logical, rational, reasonable sense—to hold off until the spring and until the prices drop. You have at least twenty solid and valid reasons—pieces of evidence—why this is logical and true. This is how it works, how we are all wired, so read the next statement very carefully:

Your essential Whisper is your highest voice, the voice of truth. The sensations and the Six Distinct Experiences are a guide to hearing that voice and knowing the truth. So please pay close attention, because the ways we resist this voice and ignore this voice are the very reasons why we claim we cannot hear this voice.

The Nature of Belief

The Whisper's voice (sensations) guides you in the present. It tells you what to do now. Your beliefs are about the past and future. Since this section is all about helping you to trust inner guidance with absolute certainty, it is important that you understand a bit about how thoughts, perceptions, and feelings form the network of your belief system.

Growing up you developed a worldview about reality. Beliefs about what reality is and what it isn't. Beliefs about how you fit into that picture, what your role is, and how you define yourself. All of this is defined by how you've perceived your experiences throughout your life.

Most beliefs are passed on to us by our peers, parents, society, community, tribe, friends, co-workers, and teachers. Very simply, we are told what to believe, and so we do. We don't always know to question our beliefs, as when LaRue was told she couldn't sing. We accept what we are told at an early age as being the truth.

~~~~~~~~~~~~~

My father was known in the countryside for finding water wells, and if anyone needed to dig a well, they would call my dad, because he could hit water every time. You know what he did? He went out to a peach tree and cut himself a branch shaped like a Y. He'd make a split in the end of the single straight branch and insert a quarter. He would hold the branch in both hands, and he'd have the straight part at the tip of the Y pointing straight out in front of him angled slightly upward at a forty-five-degree angle.

He would walk across the land, and when he found water, the tip of that branch with the quarter in it would go straight down and point toward the ground. As a child, I learned about this gift my dad had, and I remember how others talked as if my dad had this power and no one else had it. So no one else tried finding water. The other men in the countryside would doubt their ability; consequently, they weren't quite sure they could do this. They'd say, "Let's call Mr. Eppler and see if he can find water for us." My dad, taught by his father-in-law, Grandpa Hackler, however, had a real certainty in it.

~~~~~~~~~~~~~

Choose to trust and know you can absolutely develop the ability and confidence to receive your inner messages. The sensations are the divining rod. They point to truth every time and have a distinctive quality to them. You must develop a certainty in this, which comes from the practice of acting on these sensations when they arise in you.

The Purpose of Belief

The purpose of a belief is to alert you, through your feelings of peace or stress, whether what you perceive as true connects you to inner guidance or moves you away from it.

> **A belief is only useful and beneficial if it connects you to inner guidance. You will know this by becoming aware of your inner feelings, sensations, energy shifts, and the symptoms of resistance.**

We'll cover the symptoms of resistance in just a bit, but first let's take a look at some of the most common beliefs people have about recognizing, trusting, and following internal guidance. As you review the list, see if any of these are statements you've told yourself.

- Hearing the soul's voice is for special people.
- There is no such thing as being able to talk to our internal guidance.

- Suppose I am told to do something that I don't want to do.
- It takes too much work (practice) to do this.
- I am not doing this right.
- I'll never be able to do this.
- My friends (family, co-workers, etc) will think I'm crazy.
- I'll never be able to quiet my mind enough.
- I don't trust this. This can't be trusted.
- This goes against my religion.
- Only special people, ministers, priests, and rabbis can talk to God.
- My mind is too active.
- If I can hear from my soul then why do I have pain?
- This is nuts.
- I have to do this perfectly.
- I don't know what I am doing.
- Suppose the devil talks to me.
- This is confusing.
- It is safer to just do what I've been doing.
- I don't need to listen to the soul.
- I can figure out my own problems.
- I'm not ready yet.
- I'll never change.
- It doesn't matter; my life will never change.
- I can't get what I want.
- I never get what I want.
- Why would God talk to me?

These are some of the beliefs that will block you from hearing inner guidance. Did you recognize any of these? The belief statements above are just a sample of the hundreds of beliefs that any of us might hold that can sabotage our efforts in developing a partnership with inner guidance.

To the believer, these beliefs will feel very true. To someone else, these very same beliefs will have no validity. To another person, some of these beliefs will feel true while others will not. No two people have the same belief system. No two people share the same world view. Yet, even with restrictive thoughts running around in your head, the *essential, vital, and inherent* Whisper does not stop talking to you.

> **The simple test: ask yourself how you feel when you think a thought. If you feel discomfort, tension, anger, pain, irritability, resentment, shame, guilt, sadness, worry, or fear, you have a belief that is stressful and not true. This is the Whisper's way of letting you know that you are not listening. This is your way of letting you know you are not listening.**

Feelings are communication devices that let us know if we are connecting with inner guidance or moving away from inner guidance—moving toward love or blocking our awareness of it. When we are on course, we feel energized, in sync, balanced, aligned, peaceful, inspired, and loving. When we have veered off course and have moved away from our guidance, we feel discomfort and constriction. Discomfort can be felt strongly, or it can be very subtle, as with slight anxiety, worry, or tightness in the belly.

Consider all *feelings within* to be your compass. The inner sensations of the Whisper are always accompanied by the feelings or sense of spaciousness, openness, and internal peace. Strong negative emotions, such as anger, resentment, irritation, frustration, jealousy, hatred, and fear, are the absence of those qualities and act as your alarm, saying, "You are going the wrong way!" You are not placing your attention on the sensations of guidance.

The limitless truth of your soul resides in this moment, now. Your Whisper gives guidance in the moment, not in the future or in the past. The Whisper does not tell you what you should do in the future or what you should have done in the past. A life lived moment to moment has no struggle in it. Your Whisper tells you what is essential now. If you do not know what to do about something, you can ask for guidance. You can ask or say, "Show me what to do" or "What do I do next?" That is it. Get quiet and wait for your Whisper to offer your next step. Your next step simply shows up, and that is what to put your attention on.

You might receive an Urge to take a walk or to get up and wash the laundry. You might have a memory pop in of a Snapshot moment, and it clicks for you. Immediately, you get the significance of the memory and you know what to do next. If you have to make a decision about something, perhaps in your work, and you do not know what to do, you can rephrase it as a Wonder statement and wonder, "I wonder how I can handle this." You do not have to analyze what to do. When you wonder, you release the need to figure out the answer. You take yourself to the wisdom of your soul.

You open up to the limitless possibilities when you partner with the Whisper, which has access to an infinite source. Try these ideas on any of the beliefs you have that block you from hearing your Whisper. Ask your Whisper to guide you, place your attention on receiving the sensations, and watch the magic happen.

The Duality of Belief

All beliefs are limiting, even the so-called positive ones. They are a function of our world view, perceptions, and experiences. Perceptions are limited. You can only see what you see, know what you know. The mind operates within that field of knowledge, which is very limited, to say the least. Some beliefs are considered more empowering than others and less stressful, yet all beliefs are limited to some extent.

This is because all belief is dual in nature. Where there is an up, there is a down. Where there is a right, there is a wrong. In order to believe one thing, you must also have a belief that its opposite exists. For example, if you believe money is easy to make, which to some people would be considered *a positive* belief, then the opposite belief, money is hard to make, is a belief you hold true, as well, at least sometimes. Money may be easy for you to make doing a particular job, but would be considered hard to make doing another kind of job. For one person, sales may be considered an easy way to make money, while for that same person, accounting would be a hard way to make money.

The dual nature of belief is what makes it tricky to recognize when you may be resisting or ignoring your Whisper. Resistance to anything arises from holding a belief that resists or pushes you away from its opposite. If you hold the belief "I can't make money easily," then any idea or opportunity that comes along where making money seems *too easy* is automatically resisted or pushed away, even without sufficient examination or consideration.

All beliefs resist their opposite. If you are against war, you will resist peace. Sounds strange, doesn't it? Consider how many wars are waged to prevent war or in the name of peace. A familiar response, made by Mother Theresa when asked if she would march against the Vietnam War in 1967, was, "I will not march against anything, but if you have a march for peace, let me know." She knew that any action against something is resistance, and resistance sets up more resistance.

Nothing is separated from love. At the highest level of truth, there is no duality. Everything emanates from an infinite field of potential that can be known as love. Everything, even so-called negative thoughts and beliefs, are love's expression individualized. Love is all of it. Love is what is. Your belief is your belief if you choose it, and love would never argue with you. However, many beliefs we hold block our awareness of love—yet how could love argue with itself? Rain falls. Oceans contain fish. Hearts beat. We've named our reality: heart, fish, rain, mountains. We've accumulated lots of information and data about reality, and ultimately, everything connects us to our source of love, whether we are aware of it or not. You are connected to the highest vibration of your being, the source of your Whisper. Resistance argues, pushes, or struggles against nature or reality—the sensations of guidance.

The subject of belief is a fascinating one, albeit quite intricate, so fortunately the only thing really necessary to know is how your beliefs will always feel true to you and how that feeling is an unreliable gauge to recognizing inner guidance. So keep it simple: Six Distinct Experiences and the accompanying sensations.

Let's take a closer look at resistance and the symptoms of resistance. These are the feelings and reactions that occur whenever you are resisting or ignoring your essential guidance.

Resisting and Ignoring Your Essential Whisper

The inability to hear your Essential Whisper simplifies down to two actions:

1.   We **do** something we are not told by the Whisper to do.
2.   We **don't do** something we are told by the Whisper to do.

That's it. If you are having difficulty recognizing and trusting the Whisper, you may want to ask yourself, "Did I do what it told me to do the last time?"

We are either following the Whisper or we are resisting and ignoring the Whisper. Those are the only two actions possible. *If you have difficulty really trusting your guidance and acting on it, then you are going to love this section.* Here is where we lay it all out for you—the exact symptoms and reactions that occur whenever guidance is resisted.

The sensations of the Whisper are very distinctive and clear. They feel like an opening or expansion in the body. You feel aligned and sure. You may be infused with energy. You may have sensations of timelessness or fluidity of space. Above all, there is the distinct sensation of presence, heightened awareness of what is going on in the moment.

Resistance also comes with clear signals and feelings called symptoms. These symptoms alert you that you have a belief that is opposing the sensations of guidance. Inner guidance is not logical. Inner guidance is not analytical. Inner guidance is not limited. Logic, analysis, and limits are the domain of the thinking mind and have their place. If you receive a spontaneous Urge to move into another apartment or city, then acting on it by calling moving companies and comparing prices, services, and benefits is prudent. On the other hand, if you consider moving right now to be too expensive, even while you are experiencing the sensations of guidance, then you are using the limitations of belief to resist acting on the Urge.

What it Feels like to Resist Guidance

Here is a list of some of the *symptoms* that show up when we ignore or resist following the gentle guidance of our internal voice:

- Discomfort or stressful feelings, such as tightness and tension
- Constriction
- Feeling of being stuck, indecisive
- Lethargy, tiredness, lack of energy, or chronic fatigue
- Depression, melancholy, sadness
- Feeling of loss
- Pain
- Guilt
- Loneliness
- Aggressiveness
- Anger
- Irritability
- Resentment
- Incessant mind chatter (noisy thoughts)
- Feeling of being overwhelmed

These symptoms are like an alarm going off, telling you that you have moved away from your essential nature of peace. Peace is your divining rod.

～～～～～～～～～～～～～～～～～

Not long ago, I went to one of those mega shopping malls with a friend. I had a nice time browsing through the stores and talking with my friend. And then I heard within me, "Leave the mall," and felt the Urge to leave. I wasn't surprised because malls like this usually zap my energy after a while. My friend, however, wanted to continue shopping, so I ignored the message to leave and go home.

Within minutes, I became very tired, even irritable. I finally left a full hour later, and for the remainder of the day, I was cranky, tired, and just totally depleted.

- - - - - - - - - - - - - - - - - -

Remember the *one decision* and the *one action* that allows you to experience trust with certainty discussed earlier? The one decision is to decide to be aware of the sensations, and the one action is to acknowledge the sensations. Here's an easy way to understand how we resist and ignore the Whisper.

Ignoring: This is when we *refuse* to open our awareness and tune in to the sensations (conscious choice, attention, intention, and noticing).

When we *ignore* the Essential Whisper, we:

- Refuse to notice
- Pay no attention to the sensations
- Disregard
- Pay no heed and act without serious consideration of advice or messages
- Overlook
- Discount

Resisting: This is when we do not acknowledge the sensations as valid, so we are unwilling to accept or obey our guidance.

When we *resist* the Essential Whisper, we:

- Have an agenda running; there is an attachment to a particular outcome
- Can't make sense of the intuitive information and disregard it or fight it with analysis
- Really don't want to follow the voice; we want to do the same thing we always have done because it feels more comfortable
- Believe we have to give up something, i.e., free will
- Perceive a loss of control
- Believe we have to sacrifice something
- Fear giving our power away
- Would rather be right than have peace

- Get the guidance in the form of hearing, feeling or seeing, but don't trust it

Resistance will make even the simplest actions feel like struggle or effort.

~~~~~~~~~~~~~~~~~~~~~

Several years ago, back in 1993, I hosted Byron Katie, who was teaching an inquiry process she calls The Work.[2] This remarkable process has grown from a grass roots movement starting out in living rooms to an international phenomenon. The Work is detailed in her book, Loving What Is.

On one of her visits, it was particularly windy, not uncommon in Dallas. We were leaving my house to get to the car. The whipping wind was so strong that it grabbed the front door, and I had to use both hands to heave it shut. As I stumbled to the car, I tried to block the wind. I put my head down, covered my face with my arms, and ran to get into the car. In the car, I sat exhausted from fighting the strong gusts. Breathing heavily, I looked around to see where Katie was.

With a smile on her face, head thrust backward, and eyes closed, Katie stood there with her arms wide open to the sides, like wings. Her hair and clothes were being tossed around in the wind, and she just stood there. Finally, she walked over and climbed into the car, exclaiming, "I just love the wind!"

Not me! I resisted the wind. I used my strength to fend it off and climbed into the car, winded, while Katie remained refreshed and exuberant. It was a powerful lesson.

~~~~~~~~~~~~~~~~~~~~~

How to Recognize Resistance

When we are moved to a certain action by the Whisper, either through an Urge or Inspiration, for example, we are given resources of energy to complete the action. Energy is depleted when the Urge or the sensations are ignored or resisted. We may feel this as a loss of motivation or we may feel just plain tired. Doing something that directly opposes your Whisper results in an energy drain, as well. You may become tired, lethargic, and irritable. Resistance depletes energy.

Resistance has a certain feel to it. An experience of resistance is fairly easy to find. To locate a time you resisted your guidance, follow these steps:

1. Place your attention on a time when you felt a sudden drop in energy or a sudden feeling of tiredness or irritation.

2. Alternatively, if a memory doesn't show up, then find a current situation in your life where you feel stuck or indecisive.

3. Now go back to that time in your memory (or the situation you currently have) as if you are rewinding a movie, and see if you can find the moment when your energy fell. Are you there? What were you not doing that you told yourself to do?

4. Now go back until you can find the sensations that whispered what to do. Was it a subtle Urge or an inspired idea?

5. If you can go to the exact moment when the message came in, where were you? How did it feel? What was your very next thought? Did you argue with or ignore the message?

6. Write this information down in your journal or notebook. This is a clue as to the particular way you resist your Essential Whisper.

Once you know the specific symptoms and sensations of resistance, you can always know when you are in resistance!

To give you even more ways to know with certainty how to recognize resistance, we have provided a list below that tells you the symptoms of resistance for each of the Six Distinctive Experiences.

When we resist Snapshot-Click, we feel

- Separated
- Alone
- Abandoned

When we resist Collapsed Time, we experience

- Fear of death
- Fear of the past
- Obsessive behaviors
- Busyness

When we resist Collapsed Space, we feel

- Distracted
- Lost

When we resist Urge, we feel

- A sudden energy drop

- Tension (headache)
- Regret (go into "I should have")
- Distrusting of self
- Guilt

When we resist Wonderment, we feel

- Analytical
- Sad
- Hopeless
- Stingy, frugal
- Tightly focused (narrow-minded)
- Our prayers are unanswered
- Suicidal

When we resist Knowing, we experience

- Confusion
- Doubt
- Uncertainty
- Fear about future
- Panic attacks/nervousness
- Defensiveness (rightness)
- Attempts to justify our actions

When we resist Inspiration, we experience

- Lethargy/energy drain
- Depression
- Abdominal issues (second chakra)
- Loss of self-esteem
- Manic-depression (splits in personality)

These are not psychological diagnoses but rather the symptoms of resistance. If any of the above are chronic or long-term states, please seek professional help or an Evo-K facilitator.[3]

Circle or highlight any symptoms you may presently have. Go to when you first noticed the symptoms. Get quiet. What was going on? Ask, "What did I receive from the Whisper that I ignored or avoided?"

Resistance is a powerful and valuable message to you. It tells you when you are out of alignment with your natural vibration. We refer to this natural vibration and essential nature as your *intrinsic design*. This is the vital blueprint for your life and is your individualized expression. Read on to uncover your intrinsic blueprint.

It has taken a lifetime for me to learn to trust my inner knowing, my Whisper. It came through abandoning my judgment and truth as a child. For me, it began by doubting myself, which led to the blocking of my Whisper. It sometimes happens when children become outer-directed. I started listening to my older brother and people whom I thought were wiser than me. After all, if I followed their direction and suggestions and they were wrong, well, it wasn't my fault, right?

When you are afraid of not being perfect and making a mistake, you tend to take the easy way out—the irresponsible, "make up excuses" way. You make excuses for not getting everything right. So you let other people make your decisions in life, many that do not work for you, but as I said earlier, "It wasn't my fault." I started blocking my Whisper. The boys in the back room of my mind would justify why I should not listen to my own wisdom. Eventually, I overrode my Whisper with thoughts of doubt so often that I would just snuff it out like putting out a candle light.

One day, I woke up and wanted to be my authentic self. It took a conscious awareness to redevelop a trusting relationship with myself, to find my real truth. Like getting in physical shape at a gym, it took daily practice to learn to reactivate the real me.

I learned to set conscious intentions for what I wanted, and to be still and listen for direction. I remember LaRue asking me what I really wanted in life. It didn't take long to know I wanted *peace* and *clarity*. Peace of mind with my decisions, without needing to ask other people for their opinions about *my* life. Peace of mind that whatever rocked my boat would be temporary and when I got still and listened, I would find the perfect solution.

The peace thing has been huge. I used to be so inclined to accept guilt, and if something happened, I would instantly doubt myself and accept that it must have been my fault. I used to get this sick feeling and knot in my stomach and drop into a little ball of fear. The other day, I got a bank statement, and I knew I had a lot of money in the account, and yet it showed $354. I noticed I didn't crash. No little ball of fear. My inner being knew different. My first thought was, *I don't know what happened, but I have some money in savings to run the business and I can make more.* I was so peaceful about it all. I continued to look over the statement and saw the account number belonged to my operations manager's small account for incidental expenses, not my primary account. I was so amazed that I didn't panic. No little ball of fear—instead, just peace.

I also wanted *clarity*—clarity in recognizing when the Whisper was guiding me and going with those natural thoughts, even if they differed with the way someone else would have handled the situation. That became clear with a customer in Malaysia who was sent the wrong product in his order. I reviewed the situation and became peacefully still and listened. Instantly, the thought arose to replace the order with the right products and let him keep the other as a gift and possibly get him interested in using more of our products. He was so happy, and I was able to let go of money fears because I know I can always make more money. Just do the right things, follow your inner guidance, and trust it will all be well.

Peace of mind and clarity—that is what listening to my Whisper has given me. When I hear that first whispered thought, I go with it, trusting it will result in the perfect solution. Your Whisper is effortless knowledge from your highest source. Shh … be still and listen.

Perry Arledge, Kyle, TX

CHAPTER 12

➤ Your Intrinsic Design ◆

There's a Blueprint in You

Have you ever wondered what unique purpose you are here to serve? Do you notice how you gravitate toward some ideas or activities and move away from others? Do you ever have the deep feeling you are here to do some particular thing?

That's what this chapter is about: the individualized way you are designed and how your guidance system acts as a compass, pointing you to express the full potential of that design. You will also discover how resistance is established. You know what the symptoms of resistance are now, and you may have uncovered how you have ignored or resisted guidance, but have you wondered why you would resist your own guidance system? After all, isn't the Whisper guiding us toward the full expression of our gifts, talents, and desires? Why in the world would we sabotage this natural flow of love? You'll discover how to unlock the core or essential values you have that drive your behaviors and predispositions that align with your essence, as well as unmask the beliefs that get in the way and thwart your efforts. It's the great mystery you will come to master. Let's begin by going inside.

The Life Force Within

Your intrinsic design is an individualized *essence print*, a spiritual or soul blueprint that supports within you certain gifts, talents, passions, values, experiences, and ways of being in this world. It's the life force within you, expressing outwardly the essential values and core dispositions that make you come alive! It is what you are naturally: the unadulterated no-artificial-ingredients you.

This inherent pattern is your individualized life print or blueprint, which is fundamental and built in. *Individualized* does not mean separate or apart from, but rather, distinct and unique. You are an individualized aspect of the source, also known as the field of potential or consciousness. Your intrinsic design, like a fingerprint, is uniquely yours and contains within it an *energetic structure* that enables you to live your life according to your divine purpose. You express an inherently unique way of being in the world. This is similar to snowflakes; each is a magnificent beauty, perfectly formed and distinctly unique, with no other like it. No snowflake is better than another, and no snowflake is separate from snow, yet each has its own particular shape and perfection. In this way, your intrinsic design is like a snowflake.

~~~~~~~~~~~~~~~~~~~

This image of the soul print came to me in a dream. Dreams are one of the major means my soul interacts with me. It seems I am soul-printed, for example, to hear messages from my soul most clearly in dreams. There was an image of an originating radiant light source. The meaning of this light given to me inside this dream is what I would call God. Pieces of this radiating light source became individualized light, which is what I call the soul. This individualized light formed a kind of matrix or pattern that is the soul print. This soul print, like an architectural blueprint, represents the potential form of the building or the mind that houses awareness. This light radiates out farther but never disconnects from the originating source of light, and becomes the part of mind that filters awareness and holds the values, beliefs, perceptions, and preferences that support the life purpose of the individual. As the soul's light shines through these filters, in this part of mind, the beliefs and values create personality and life experiences.

~~~~~~~~~~~~~~~~~~~

The dream and its description show that perhaps there is an individualized expression of a source of potentiality, which actualizes through each of us. We are the expression of an individualized piece of light. Some call this design of light and energy *the matrix*. This matrix of light—this individualized and inherent pattern within us—manifests as expression. This matrix connects us all and is the substance that intelligence (consciousness) flows through.

Greg Braden writes in his book, *The Divine Matrix*, "Experiments demonstrate that there's a power within each of us that's unlike any ever created by a machine in a laboratory. It's a force that's not bound by the laws of physics—at least not the ones we understand today. And we don't need a lab experiment to know that this connection exists."[1]

Scientists are discovering that the whole universe is a matrix of energy, a highway system, so to speak, of energy and intelligence, and that we are all connected along this matrix, this web of design. This matrix individualizes into distinct energy signatures, and you are a distinct energy signature within this field we call your intrinsic design. This is the essence of your being and the source of your Essential Whisper.

Your Life Purpose is Built In

Your life purpose is not what you are *supposed* to do or accomplish, but rather what you are *naturally designed* to be. It is the way you incorporate your unique gifts and talents into who you are.

You are automatically and naturally attracted to the people and situations that resonate with your intrinsic design. What you are naturally attracted to is a reflection of what is inside you, your energy signature. You do not need to run around trying to figure out your life purpose. It sits within and continually whispers to you through the distinct sensations that alert you to what attracts you and what doesn't. Your heartfelt desires rise spontaneously in response to what is next in your life. These desires are presented to you through the six experiences and sensations of your Whisper. You'll get to dive deeper into this in the next chapter. For now, it's important to understand how your values and beliefs either align with or don't align with your intrinsic design.

There are particular beliefs and values that are supported by and arise from your intrinsic design. These intrinsic values support the expression of your life purpose within you. The questions that opened this chapter—Have you ever wondered what unique purpose you are here to serve? Do you notice how you gravitate toward some ideas or activities and move away from others? Do you ever have the deep feeling you are here to be some particular thing?—they are answered through your intrinsic design. You have an energetic program that resonates and aligns with the beliefs and values that support the full expression of your intrinsic design and life purpose. This is why—in part, at least—you gravitate toward very particular ideas and experiences. Your intrinsic design is the creative element of your being.

Try this. To get started uncovering your intrinsic design, take a few moments and answer these questions:

- **What are your gifts?** These are the natural inclinations you have, such as the gift of conversation or the gift of humor or the gift to motivate.

- **What are your talents?** These are the natural skills you possess, such as the talent to sing or the talent to write stories.

- **What are your passions?** This is why you express your gifts and talents in a particular way. If you have the gift to motivate and the talent to sing, you may have a strong passion to sing uplifting and motivational songs in elder-care homes to bring joy to shut-ins.

Go ahead; get a cup of tea or soothing beverage and then get still for a few moments, breathing deeply while you answer these questions. You may be amazed at what you discover. Begin placing your attention on how you move and express yourself in the world. The beautiful part of this is you are giving yourself the opportunity to reveal what intrinsically lies within as the perfect unfolding of your creative design.

Your Values and Beliefs

As you study yourself and become your very own experiment, you will become more and more aware of what you believe and think to be true. It's a fascinating study that can be embraced with the enthusiasm of a kid digging for bugs and exploring her environment. Everything is new, alive, and filled with wonder. So take it on as the extraordinary experiment of you. Why not? You are operating from your deepest beliefs and values, anyway; might as well learn what they are.

Values are those beliefs that are extremely important to us and motivate our behavior. They are so important that we would die or fight to maintain them rather than release or change them. They are the foundation underpinning our actions and are what we ultimately create in our lives. Values underlie our decisions, behaviors, and all of our other beliefs. This makes values a pretty important part of who we determine ourselves to be! Values, very simply, determine our identity. We are what we value. Or so we believe!

Actually, what you are is essence. The fundamental nature of you is spirit, life energy, an individualized signature of love. Your soul's purpose (if it is claimed to have one) is the expression of this essence into what we know as the material world, the world of form and substance. When we are truly living in alignment with our essence, we move as one with it. There is no editing between the occurrence of sensation and the movement that expresses that sensation. Another way to say this is: love says do the dishes, and even before that thought is finished, there is movement toward the dishes, and then the inner sensations guide the next move.

Editing is the function of our mind, the part of self, that contains the beliefs and values we hold dear. The sensation of guidance is beyond belief and is felt from our individualized essence. If the guidance we receive doesn't contradict a belief or value we have, then we are more likely to follow that guidance. If the guidance we receive does contradict a belief or value we have, then we are more likely to resist the guidance and edit the message.

This is where resistance to inner guidance comes from. The mind edits the information and governs what is true and what is not true based on the belief and value system in place. If your guidance system tells you to look at new houses, and your mind edits with "This is a seller's market. I'll never find a good deal. I'll wait until the market changes," because you have a belief that good deals don't exist in a seller's market, then it is unlikely you will follow your guidance urging you to look at new houses.

The sensations of inner guidance *align* with your intrinsic design. Arguing with these sensations is akin to arguing with your very own essential nature. This is why so many people are unable to attract their heartfelt desires. The desire rises up from the intrinsic design, fills you with the sensations of openness and energy, jettisons you in one or more of the Six Experiences, and the belief that it *can't be done* or *should happen another way* resists the guidance, the very thing you wanted.

Aligning Values and Beliefs with Your Intrinsic Design

How can we stop resistance? You've already developed values that align with your intrinsic design. Since the sensations of inner guidance align with your intrinsic design, you can stop fighting yourself and resisting your Whisper by determining the values that you hold. These are called your *intrinsic values*.

Intrinsic values are those operating beliefs that resonate with the experiences and situations in your life that most align with your life's purpose and passion. You can effortlessly attract into your life those experiences that enable you to live with zeal and passion when you get in touch with your intrinsic (core) values. Many people get stuck trying to figure out their life's purpose, as if it is some big outstanding thing they are supposed to do. Your life's purpose is built into your intrinsic design and is recognizable to you through the sensations associated with joy, peace, passion, and inspiration as well as how these sensations are expressed in your relationships and everyday life.

Intrinsic Values

The values that align with the vibration of your intrinsic pattern and motivate you to express your gifts, talents, and passion are your *intrinsic values.* If your intrinsic nature resonates with music, then you may express this outwardly through song or by playing an instrument. You would value music and encourage it in your life and the lives of those around you. Your intrinsic design supports what you deeply desire and naturally wish to express.

Values are neither inherently good nor bad. They either align with your intrinsic design or they don't.

Values are neither good nor bad. In our lives, all events and experiences are helpful. For one person, the value of creativity is very important, and she feels balanced, solid, and strong when she is doing something creative. For another person, the value of family is strong; he builds strong relationships with his family and lives his life expressing that value.

Yet the one who values creativity may love solitude, with simple, intermittent relationships. Both sets of values are balanced and true for each person, although not embodied equally by both of them.

Understanding what your values are and determining whether they align with your intrinsic blueprint is critical if you want to eliminate resisting your essential guidance.

Some key qualities of intrinsic values:

- They are the ones you desire to express.
- They resonate with your gifts and talents.
- They are uniquely yours, like a fingerprint.
- They support the beliefs that are empowering to you.
- They drive or motivate your passion.
- They mirror your intrinsic design. What is energetic and invisible as your matrix becomes visible as you create experiences.

Uncovering Your Intrinsic Values

What you are attracted to will naturally and intrinsically show up as feelings of admiration, respect, or awe. You feel admiration and deep respect and attraction toward those traits and characteristics that represent your intrinsic design.

Your intrinsic values are longing to be expressed, because they represent what you admire from the deepest place within; they mirror the feeling of awe within you. Awe is the state of being in the presence of God (inspired by the sacred or sublime). Interestingly, the word *admire* comes from the roots *ad* and *mirari*, which mean to wonder. Intrinsic values put us in a state of wonder—in a state of awe or wonderment. Isn't that awesome? But wait, it gets better. The word *mirror* is also derived from the same root as admire, *mirari*. The word *mirror* represents a reflection of God—a representation of awe.

Next time you look in *the mirror*, remember this as you look beyond the form and deeply into your own eyes! You are looking at God. You are seeing the reflection of wonder and awe, a magnificent representation of an individualized aspect of the divine.

Locating and uncovering your intrinsic values is quite easy and fun to do.

Find some quiet time, grab a pencil, and work through the following exercise.

Write down one person you admire, really admire—a person you are in awe of. Start out with just one for now, then come back and do as many as you like.

Write who it is here: _____

When we think (imagine) of those we admire, there is a sense of wonder about them. Children often admire superheroes, mythological characters, athletes, and bigger-than-life personalities. These are just as valid—it is the state of wonder that shows us what we resonate with. Admiration *echoes* the internal sense of wonder. What you admire (the value or characteristic) resonates (echoes) what you desire to express and represents your intrinsic design. What you admire, respect, and feel awe toward is mirroring your natural way of being!

So as you list who you admire, ask yourself, "Who brings me a sense of wonder? Who do I say 'Wow!' to? Who do I think is awesome, inspiring, uplifting, magical, and lovely? Who do I hold in high esteem? Who astonishes me?

Please find the one person you admire before moving to the next section.

Extrinsic Values

Your extrinsic values are outside your intrinsic design. Think of fun-house mirrors, those mirrors that are in the tents at circuses and state fairs. When you step in front of them, your image is distorted, appearing tall and thin, or short and squat. It's a distorted image of you, closely resembling you, but it is imprecise. That's the way it is with extrinsic values; they are imprecise and distorted.

As you know now, all your beliefs (anything you hold as true) compose what is called a *belief system*. Your belief system filters your perceptions, concepts, and experiences in the world and forms your identity—who you believe yourself to be. This is your interpretation of your world, your world view. You programmed in what the world *should or should not be* and how the world *should or should not think* about you. These become the *shoulds* in your life.

> **When you use the word *should*, it refers to an extrinsic value. These distorted expressions are the source of all feelings of inadequacy.**

So, to use the example of someone who has an intrinsic value of artistic creativity, she may believe that she cannot make money or live off her creativity, so she believes she *should* pursue another vocation and not waste her time. She holds the belief that being creative would limit her ability to be successful or productive or financially self-sustaining in the world. She may attempt to use her creativity in a job she really doesn't like and is unhappy in, because she believes this job allows her to be both creative *and* financially secure. The *should* distorts her intrinsic value of artistic creativity and converts it into the extrinsic value of financial security.

Freedom is a strong intrinsic value for me—freedom from limited and restrictive thinking and freedom to live life the way I want to create it. Eventually, my path led me to the people and experiences that would teach me how to live in true freedom with joy and ease. Before that happened, however, the value of freedom was distorted in my mind, and I thought it meant I needed to escape what I didn't like about my life. So, I got involved in an early marriage to escape my family, affairs to escape my marriage, men to escape the pain of divorce, and illness to escape the pervasive fear that there was something wrong with me. I was trying to find freedom living by someone else's rules. Now, instead of looking for freedom by escaping, I live my life's purpose through my intrinsic value of true freedom, embracing the fullness of life, and freely accepting all it offers.

Extrinsic values are what we think we should do or be to get us to that state of awe. We desire to have awe in our lives, to have lives filled with wonder and joy. Feelings will let you know which value you are living from.

Examples of the feelings values give us:

Intrinsic values feel	Extrinsic values feel
Awesome	Draining
Inspirational	Difficult (effort)
Motivating/energizing	Obligatory/necessary
Aligned	False, out of sync
Resonant	Unnatural, discordant

So the BIG QUESTION is, "How does the *expression* of values get distorted?" The value itself isn't distorted; it's the expression of the intrinsic value that gets distorted.

The value of financial security isn't any better than the value of creativity. It's that the intrinsic value of creativity in the example above became distorted and is being *expressed as* financial security instead of creativity. As you stand in front of those fun-house mirrors, your actual body isn't distorted; the image reflected is distorted. Same body, distorted image.

Uncovering Your Extrinsic Values

The purpose of reviewing and revealing your values is so that you can recognize how you may resist your essential guidance and not even know it. Shining light on the way values operate in your life will make it so much easier for you to notice the symptoms of resistance and locate the belief that is getting in the way. Let's take a peek at how your extrinsic values may substitute for your intrinsic value and represent the *shoulds* in your life. Ready?

Find a few more moments of quiet time, grab that same pencil, and work through the following exercise.

1. Use the person you wrote above, who you deeply and respectfully admire. Write the quality or characteristic about them that you admire the most. (You can come back later and write several more.) _____

Example: Oprah. I admire that she walks her talk.

2. Fill in the statement "I want to" with the quality.

   I want to (be, express) _____

Example: I want to walk my talk.

   3.   What would you have to do in order to express the quality you listed in #2?

List everything you can think of that you believe you'd have to be or do to have the quality you admire.

In order for me to _____, I would have to (be, do, have)

_____

_____

_____

Example: In order for me to walk my talk I would have to:

Censor what I say
Not make any mistakes
Be an expert on my subject
Always tell the truth
Be perfect
Be on guard (careful what I say)
Follow through and follow-up

   4.   The list above shows you what you believe you have to do, and how you would have to change in order to express the quality you admire. For the world to see me as someone who _____, I would have to _____

Example: For the world to see me as someone who walks my talk, I would have to be on guard and be careful what I say.

   5.   Go through each one on your list and ask, "How does it feel inside to _____"?

Example: How does it feel to be on guard and careful what I say? It feels false and dishonest. Hmmm, not exactly walking the talk!

Are the feelings you listed the sensations of the Whisper or something else?

Using the example above, the intrinsic value "walk my talk" (being authentic, honest) gets distorted by the beliefs of what it would take to do that, how it *should* happen. In this example, be on guard is the extrinsic value. In truth, the Whisper will guide you in limitless ways to walk your talk. If you admire it, resonate with it, see yourself doing it, then, it is in your intrinsic blueprint. There's nothing you *have to do* to manifest that value in your life.

As you fill in these statements, what feelings do you feel? These *shoulds* are some of your distorted, extrinsic values, and because they are valued, they motivate and unconsciously drive your choices and decisions. Again, they are neither good nor bad, but if they are not in alignment with your inherent values—those values you truly want to express in your life—you will have feelings of inadequacy, doubt, and fear as you attempt to live your life through them. Take a look at your list above. How do you make decisions using those values? What do you do to make sure the world sees you a certain way? Using the examples above, the response might be, "To make sure the world sees me as someone who walks my talk, I am very careful about what I say."

Go through each one, as you have time and desire, and study yourself. As you become aware of the ways you have tried to live your life by someone else's values (shoulds) you will find it harder and harder to resist the Whisper. You will come to know your essential guidance as the deepest alignment with what and who you are. Imagine how much easier it will be now to live your life in harmony with your essential blueprint.

The wonderful thing about values is they show you why you behave the way you do. Get in the habit of asking yourself how a certain behavior reflects a value you have.

What you do in your life right now, what you have in your life right now, and what you put your attention and energy on in your life right now is what you value.

If you are telling yourself you value being financially secure, yet you are not saving any money or learning about investments or reading business journals and money management books, or if you are spending more money than you have, then your attention and actions are not aligned with the value of financial security. In reality, you do not value it, and it doesn't represent a particular strength or gift you have. Rather than make yourself value what you do not and make yourself wrong for not living what you think you should value, take a look at what you are putting your attention on. What is it in your life that feels awesome, aligned, and energizing, and that resonates? Perhaps financial security isn't your value after all, and you really value travel. Travel inspires you. You would spend your last dime visiting exotic out-of-the-way countries learning about other cultures!

~~~~~~~~~~~~~~~~~~~~

For years, I wanted the world to think I was authentic. I spent much of the time pretending to be outgoing, happy, fun-loving, and just plain okay, all the while feeling shy, scared, and unsure of myself, wanting others to love and approve of me. So I faked authenticity, because I wanted people to see me as authentic. Pretty crazy, huh?

Being me without pretending anything is authentic, and being me is intrinsically perfect. So now, I admit my shyness when I feel it. I admit when I don't know the answer to something or when I am not feeling fun-loving and would prefer a quiet evening at home.

~~~~~~~~~~~~~~~~~~~~~~

Your intrinsic values show you your *intrinsic perfection*; they match your unique design, your unique way of being. It is not necessary to go to the world to validate these values. Who you really are sits within you, perfectly available. They are what you *know* is true about you, and you can *trust* these implicitly.

Now that you know how to uncover your intrinsic blueprint and the values that support it, you are ready to attract your heartfelt desires.

CHAPTER 13

❧ Attract Your Heartfelt Desires with Certainty ❦
Allow the Whisper to Do the Work

Your heartfelt desires arise spontaneously and instinctively. Felt internally, desires are merged with one of the Six Distinct Experiences and the sensations of guidance. They do not need to be conjured up. It is not necessary to make them up or to imagine them, draw up vision boards or write them out. When you are hit with a spontaneous desire, it is given to you clearly, distinctly, and in full living color. True desires are born from the heart and soul, what you have come to know as your intrinsic design.

Your intrinsic design—your life blueprint—holds the matrix of what you are here to express. It is your piece of the unlimited field of potential. This is fabulous to know. Consider this: all that you truly desire and hope for, all that you are truly attracted to and resonate with, all that you are truly aligned with and intrinsically designed for, is yours for the asking. But the question is, can you trust the guidance that leads you to what you desire?

- -

The first time I was aware of this happening was about twenty-five years ago. I was living on a military base in South Carolina with my husband, and occasionally I would pass this beautiful furniture store. I never shopped at this store, because I didn't have the money, but I would go after closing and look in the window and dream.

One evening after closing, I peeked through the front door, and down the aisle on the left was the most gorgeous sofa table I had ever seen. It was made of this beautiful wood and was quite expensive, and I just loved it. I had a real heartfelt desire for this table. I wouldn't have used these words back then, because I didn't know them, but there was an energy that drew me to this table, and I would think about it and think about it, all the while believing I couldn't afford it.

One day, after my bonus check arrived for $550, I worked up the courage to approach the salesperson. The table was selling for several hundred dollars more than I had, but I said, "If you sell this table to me for $550 exactly and deliver it, I will buy it."

The salesperson left to get the manager, and when the manager returned, he said, "When do you want it delivered?

Wow! I could really have this? The table was going on sale that day for the exact amount of money I had. It was the first time I had ever made the connection between a heartfelt desire, a real yearning for something, and actually getting it. This was when I began to realize it wasn't just a coincidence, an accident, or a fluke … my desire could be actually manifested and brought to me.

Your Natural Desires

You heartfelt desires, those inner yearnings, are a natural expression of your intrinsic gifts and strengths. In other words, what you desire, as it arises from your heart and inner being, you are able to manifest when you trust and follow the inner sensations and distinct experiences presented to you. If you've been unable to fulfill your desires, it may be that your belief system says, "This is not the way it's supposed to look." You could spend your whole life feeling like a failure, even though you have been given guidance toward your heartfelt requests all along.

One of these spiritual laws has been written about quite extensively. In books like *The Secret* by Rhonda Byrne [1] and in *Ask and It is Given* by Esther and Jerry Hicks,[2] you can read more about what is referred to as *the law of attraction*. Recently, *The Secret* became a major DVD phenomenon, clarifying and elucidating this principle in a new and fresh way. The movie presents validating information from the field of quantum physics, as well as the personal anecdotes from contemporary celebrities, authors, doctors, writers, and many other familiar personalities.

The law of attraction, however, isn't new, and it isn't merely a whimsical technique. Attraction is continuously ongoing, regardless of your conscious participation in it. In other words, you are always attracting to you the experiences that match your state of being, beliefs, and attention. Do you recall back in Chapter 8 the discussion on manifestation? Here's a quick summary:

- **All beliefs are formed emotionally**; they are based on the *perceived evidence* we have for the belief.

- **You've already given yourself evidence for every belief and value you hold,** so every single one *feels true,* whether it aligns with your intrinsic design or not.

- **To manifest anything is to make it evident**, which means the object or experience becomes readily perceived by the senses and easily understood or recognized by the mind. In other words, what we see, we've created—we've made manifest.

- **You are doing the manifesting.** To manifest is to make something perceptually evident. Manifesting is *you giving you* evidence of something.

Here's the problem with trying to understand the law of attraction, as it is sometimes described. It appears that you attract and bring to you what you place your attention on.

You are always creating (manifesting) either in alignment, or out of alignment, to your intrinsic design. The universe simply complies, and it looks as though what you've created and experienced was brought to you from somewhere else. Yet creating happens right here, right now. Manifesting is not a future phenomenon. All you need is always given in each present moment; nothing is withheld.

There is indeed a spiritual law in place—in fact, several. And knowing these laws and operating within their parameters will provide additional insight as to how to experience the life that aligns with your essence, and either of the sources mentioned earlier will be valuable resources to you to do this. But the easiest way to live a life that fully aligns with your essential nature is to follow the sensations, which already spring from and are woven into your individualized matrix, your Essential Whisper.

A spontaneous desire is a natural desire. It is not a desire that is constructed mentally by you. You do not have to think about it or ponder it or make it up. It arises from within, sometimes quite suddenly. Spontaneous desire rivets your attention on a particular item, experience, or goal. Usually, we are told to formulate our plans, map out a vision board, and paste on it pictures of what we want. We are told to imagine our goals clearly and place our attention on the desire so that we can attract it to us. A spontaneous desire requires no such effort, and in fact, it is hard to take your attention off of what arises instinctively from within.

Creating an intentional desire is fine, but you may not get what you think you want if what you think you want isn't what you really want. Is that confusing? Exactly! Here is what can happen when you make up what you think you want:

You may be trying to design your life from your belief system instead of from your intrinsic design.

This is why so many feel they have failed. So much of what we tell ourselves we want to possess or experience is not in our individualized intrinsic life print. These desires are what the world (our friends, family, colleagues, etc.) tells us it values, how we should be, and what we should have. These wishes may not be what you really, really want in your heart.

By trying to live your life according to someone else's values, you will struggle and attempt with great effort to grasp joy as it continues to elude you, moving just out of your reach. This is living from the *extrinsic values*, which produce a distorted self-image—metaphorically, the body in the fun-house mirror. This is not living from your heart and soul, but rather from *shoulds*. Here's what living from *should* looks like: you try to determine the right course of action to take, the right people to associate with, the right books and classes to study, the right foods to eat, the right clothes to wear, the right words to speak, the right amount of money to make, and so forth.

From this point forward, make a promise to yourself. Promise yourself that you are going to live intrinsically aligned. You are going to trust the magnificent essential nature of you. You are going to manifest your heartfelt desires, starting right now. Starting right now, you are going to trust your Essential Whisper to guide you toward the fulfillment of your spontaneous and natural desires. Here's how.

Let the Whisper Do the Work

Inner guidance *is* the law. It wears the sheriff's badge. Break the law, go to jail. In this case, that would be the jail of struggle and effort, the bars of resistance. Follow the law and experience freedom, freedom from the exertion of trying to figure out your life and trying to determine if you are doing the right thing or the best thing. Freedom is what living in the present moment is all about.

The sensations of inner guidance, the inner feeling of expansion or contraction, operate within the law. This is exactly why you can have certainty in this. Your intrinsic design is a matrix of energy that responds to your thoughts. Expansive and aligning thoughts bring about the sensation of expansion, openness, spaciousness, peace, presence, and energy. Discordant and misaligned thoughts and beliefs will show up as stress, constriction, and tightness. That's the law. Even if you aren't sure if a thought or belief you have is aligned or misaligned with your intrinsic print, you can simply hold the thought in mind, breathe, and notice what sensations arise within.

Spontaneous desires arrive with an idea or thought of something you would like to have or do. This idea or thought resonates with something within your intrinsic design ready to be expressed. When you get a spontaneous, heartfelt desire, you are filled with energy, aliveness, even laughter. It's a definite *yes!* That's how you know what you *really* want. But here's the best part: these sensations continue to guide you toward the manifestation of that desire. As you follow the distinct experiences that may show up (Urge, Snapshots, Inspiration, and so forth) along with the sensations, you are lead, step by step, to unfolding that desire.

~ ~ ~ ~ ~ ~ ~ ~ ~ ~ ~ ~ ~ ~ ~ ~ ~ ~

A couple of years ago, I set out to paint a small chest I had in my living room. I had four days off, and I knew if I didn't get it done within that time, it wouldn't get done for months. I painted the drawers using a water-based paint, and the drawers swelled from the water. Since I really wanted to finish painting, I thought about buying a sander. Funny thing, as I traveled to the neighborhood Home Depot, I felt a sudden Urge to go to the one in the next community several miles away.

In the store, I was thinking, I do need a sander today, but I probably won't use it again for ten years. *I had always wanted a sander for various projects, yet it didn't make a lot of sense for me to buy one. So I figured I would run in, select one, and get out of there. There were a lot of sanders. Shelves filled with various sizes, models, accessories. This was going to be harder than I thought.*

A voice behind me said, "I wouldn't buy one of those if I was you. You can just borrow mine."

There was a man standing there looking at me. Dumbfounded, I said, "You mean you would do that?"

He said, "Oh sure. I've only been burned once. Do you have more shopping to do? I only live three minutes from here. I can run home and get it for you."

I didn't have any shopping to do, so I told him I could follow him home, and as we walked to the parking lot, he stopped at his red van, which was parked literally right next to my car.

While following this man in my car, my mother's voice went off in my head. "What are you doing? Don't go off with strangers." I thought I should call my son and let him know where I was, yet I was feeling peace inside, so I just went with the peace. We pulled up to his house and he politely gestured for me to wait outside for him. The next thing I knew, these kids ran over and started talking to me. They invited me inside, and I could see he was redoing the kitchen cabinets and had to make a quick run to Home Depot for something.

I borrowed the sander, returning it a couple of days later. His wife answered the door and humorously exclaimed, "Oh you're the person who is going to help us refinish the cabinets!" I met more of the kids, and it was the sweetest thing. When I left there that day, I was in tears. It occurred to me that the universe had always answered my prayers. It had always been trying to give me what I asked for, but because of my conditioning (the shoulds and the fear-based thoughts) I was not saying yes to what I was given. Therefore, I couldn't receive it. This was a really touching moment.

How to Let the Whisper Do the Work

When you ask, "What do I want?" or when you *think about* what it is you *should* have, then you also have to think of what you want that you don't have. You are mentally conjuring up a desire from a place of lack.

A common *want* for many, for example, is to lose weight. Some look in the mirror, and, aghast, exclaim, "I've got to lose weight!" They begin fervently exercising, reading all the latest diet tips, withholding food, and reading nutrition labels in order to restrict fat and calories. All the while, thinking about how fat or out of shape they are, they yearn for certain foods. Does this sound familiar to you? Even if this isn't your personal experience, certainly you recognize that the weight management business is a multibillion-dollar industry.

Dieting, wanting my body to look differently, has been my personal experience for years! I would go on and off diets and exercise programs, eat foods I didn't like but thought I should eat, and constantly try to look a certain way to win the approval of others, namely men. Can you relate? You see, what I really wanted was to love my body, to feel strong, vibrant, and healthy. But I was attached to my beliefs and filled with the thoughts, I am fat, I am hungry, *and* I am out of shape. *I continued to perceive my body as one that I didn't like and struggled for many years.*

So suppose you do desire to lose weight; then what is the best way to attract this effortlessly? Once you know what you really want and desire, you will feel the energy of it. Just the vision of your desire will inspire you and fill you with energy. Does the thought of taking cooking classes enliven you? Have you always wanted to learn how to ski or scuba dive? Does preparing foods grown from your own garden inspire you?

To attract without effort, listen for your directions and answers, and tune into your heart's voice—your Essential Whisper. Tune into the sensations of peace, spaciousness, openness, energy, joy, and certainty that arise through the

Six Distinct Experiences of Snap-Click, Collapsed Time, Urge, Wonderment, Knowing, and Inspiration as they appear in synchronicities, conversations, dreams, and the other interactive devices for receiving information. This is how your Whisper guides you to reach your goals, although some ideas won't seem related to the goal of losing weight, such as scuba diving. How is *that* helpful? As stated earlier, we are always attracting our heartfelt desires, but if it doesn't look like we think it's supposed to look, we will discount the sensations and ignore our guidance, and perhaps miss the wonderful way scuba diving, a long-felt desire, actually helps curb appetite, takes abundant muscular strength, and regulates breathing, and is way better than counting calories.

First, place your attention on something you desire.
Let's use the above example: **I want to lose weight**.

Second, change it to a wonder statement: **I wonder what would be the best way for me to eat well, with enjoyment, and lose weight in a fun way.**

This immediately opens you up to hear options and ideas, and to see the possibilities. No need to look for these; relax and they will simply show up. Just notice and bring your attention to hearing how your soul will show you your answer.

Do you find suddenly that you are Inspired to look into yoga or join a belly dancing class? While driving, do you follow an Urge to take a right where you normally turn left, only to find a wonderful restaurant serving delicious healthy foods that you didn't know was there? Does someone mention a wonderful movie to see, and you KNOW to go see it and then find yourself sitting next to someone who invites you on a group ski trip, something you have wanted to do for a long time? Can you see how fun and effortless this is?

~~~~~~~~~~~~~~~~~~~~

Images of rapists and murderers and fearful thoughts about strangers played in my mind while I followed the SanderMan. The experience of peace I felt in my heart was stronger than the fearful noise in my head or I would not have followed him home. The sense of spaciousness was there, along with the complete feeling this was okay.

The universe was giving me what I asked for, which was a sander. Even more telling, I didn't go to the Home Depot closest to my home and instead went to one farther away. As we moved through the store and then through the parking lot, it seemed there was just the two of us … not a store … not a parking lot, just presence, as if we were in a bubble and nothing outside the bubble existed. Time collapsed.

I followed a creative inspiration to paint and then an urge to buy a sander, and I traveled to a specific store to get one. What I wanted was clear: a sander I didn't have to buy. Of course, I didn't think about not buying one as I stood there looking at all the varieties of sanders, yet the desire was very clear, and it was what my heart really wanted. In this case, unlike the experience with VitaminMan, I also had fearful thoughts going through my head. Perhaps I should call my son. *It was difficult to have the confidence I was following the sensation of peace, although I could feel it in my heart. When I don't have any illusions, fantasies, or fears going on, it's just a full knowing. The key is, I had a clear intention and was able to recognize this experience was an answer to that intention—placed right there in front of me—so I could tune out the fearful noise in my head and tune in to my heart.*

You can listen internally to the sensations of guidance even while the mind chatter is still going on. The Whisper is very distinct and continues to speak to you amidst the fearful noise in your head, but it does take practice and the developing of trust that comes with that practice to be able to discern the difference. So play with this a bit; see if you can remember when you did follow inner guidance even though you were a bit afraid.

There is no suggestion here, of course, to discount fear or a voice of warning. **Inner feelings or sensations of constriction and tightness mean wait or stop.** There are hundreds, maybe thousands, of stories of how someone walked into a dangerous situation even while they experienced very direct sensations of constriction and warning.

Inner guidance directs movement very clearly through sensations of inner peace, even when the thinking self is going wild. Is the situation happening in alignment with your intentions and desire? Do you feel openness and energy with what is happening? All that is ever required from you is to notice, to have a sincere desire to practice following inner guidance. You are never required or prompted to do what is outside your level of comprehension or ability at that moment.

So before moving to the next really fun chapter that describes in detail the various ways you will get messages and directions from inner guidance, go ahead, start playing now and try attracting your heartfelt desires, without effort.

Attract Your Heartfelt Desires *Effortlessly*

1. What do you want? What would you like to have right now in your life that you do not have? Locate the thing or experience you have a strong, heartfelt desire for or have desired for some time. Be specific and write it as an "I desire" statement.

"I really desire _____."
Example: I really desire to work with animals and make good money doing it.

2. Breathe slowly and deeply. Place your focus on your heart.

3. When relaxed restate your "I want" statement into an "I wonder" statement. Allow one to bubble up from your heart.

"Hmm … I wonder _____."

Example: hmmm…. I wonder how I will work with animals and make money with it.

4. Now let it go.

5. Pay attention to your environment and the messages that show up to point you in the direction of your desire.

You will receive messages in many ways and distinct forms of interactions. Jump to the next chapter and learn what they are.

SECTION THREE

Following Your Essential Whisper

CHAPTER 14

❧ Interactions with Your Essential Whisper ❦

Receiving Distinct Messages

Remember the sander story in the previous chapter? Did you find a similar story in your life? When you read that story, did you call it a synchronicity or coincidence?

Up until now, we have focused on the sensations felt as distinct communication from inner guidance. These are the sensations of energy, certainty, resonance, expansiveness, peace, and neutrality. We've covered, and by now you have located, the Six Distinct Ways or Experiences that give rise to these sensations. These experiences of Snapshot-Click, Collapsed Time and Space, Urge, Wonderment, Knowing, and Inspiration propel us into direct relationship with the Whisper.

You've gotten really good at discerning the Whisper, acknowledging it, and expanding your awareness of the subtle yet distinct sensations you can feel. You've practiced recognizing and trusting your guidance and have noticed and become more aware of certain beliefs that may block that trust and cause you to resist or ignore your wisdom. You have uncovered your intrinsic design and the unique gifts and talents that will enable you to express an individualized passion and purpose. You now know your heartfelt desires and allow your Whisper to do the work.

So the next step is to know how to tell what the message is—what you are being directly guided to do or act on. How do you know what is direct information from your Whisper? This entire section is devoted to helping you follow and act on your Whisper with absolute certainty. No doubt you will recognize many of the ways your Whisper interacts with you, but you may not have known that these are indeed distinct and clear messages from your soul.

~~~~~~~~~~~~~~~~~~~

For me, getting that sander in the way I did was my moment of recognition, the moment when I recognized that I had been receiving everything I asked for my whole life. I wondered how often it showed up and I didn't see it or receive it because what I asked for didn't look like what I thought it should look like. Here was the universe ready and willing to give me a sander for my little cabinet. How often did I ignore or block receiving what I desired because it didn't seem important enough or spiritual enough? After all, going to Home Depot hardly constitutes biblical mention.

~~~~~~~~~~~~~~~~~

There are very distinct ways to receive clear information and specific messages. Of course, the first and foremost way we receive information is through the sensations and feelings in the body, notably the sensations and distinguishable feelings of presence, stillness, and resonance. There are also the distinctive symptoms of resistance, namely stress and discomfort. These symptoms tell you that you missed the message. We will discuss these in more detail in the next chapter.

However, along with the internal sensations, direct communication and messages from divine guidance can arrive through the written or spoken word, highly meaningful events, your dreams, symbols, or direct internal dialogue with your Whisper.

> **Many people don't believe they can talk to inner wisdom because these simple means of communication are believed to be coincidences, flukes, insignificant, and so on. They aren't.**

It is important to mention and critical for you to understand that if you are seeking answers and guidance from motivation other than a true partnership with your Whisper, such as for personal gain at the expense of another, you will encounter some very funky answers, and ultimately, you will end up confused. To avoid confusion or mistaking emotion for sensation, be sure to keep your intentions directed on your heart. When you do this, you can have confidence to act on what you receive.

Eventually, your faith quickens and strengthens as you act on and follow your inner voice. For those times when you are not sure if you have heard from your Whisper, simply ask for a clearer response or ask an essential question or wondering. Direct your attention to the sensation. Do you feel open and expansive or doubtful with constriction and tightness? If you are not sure, don't act; simply wait,

Experiencing synchronicities, vivid dreams, and direct communication is very exciting. These manifestations, however, are not the guide, just the means of communication. Follow the Six Distinct Experiences and inner sensations, for they are your guide, not the physical appearances. In other words, you are not looking for *signs and symbols* and then trying to determine *if* you heard from your Whisper. Stay out of your head; there is no analysis in this. Remember, these physical manifestations are *always accompanied* by the distinct sensations of peace and presence felt internally.

Synchronicity: A Highly Meaningful Event

Synchronicity is a term that was coined by the eminent psychologist Carl Jung. It is defined as: *An event or series of events that appear improbable or coincidental, yet is highly significant and meaningful to the person experiencing it.*

The key word here is *significant*. You have experienced synchronistic events and most likely have many fascinating stories of the seemingly strange ways that ideas, people, and information came to you, right? Have you wondered how these came to you or how you can bring synchronicity into your life consistently and even intentionally?

Even though synchronicities occur very frequently, many think of these improbable events as interesting occurrences that happen only occasionally, by chance. Synchronicities are *not* chance encounters or fluke events. They are responses to your heartfelt desires, your wonderings, your essential questions, and your intentions. They respond to the highest measure of what you desire. Synchronicities appear consistently and very frequently once you receive them as divine messages from the Whisper. Every story in this book is a story of synchronicity. The plot seems coincidental or accidental, yet tucked within each story is the timeless element of the divine, the miraculous and the indefinable pattern of love.

Reasoning and logic won't get you to this sense of awe. Synchronicities occur outside the mental gray matter of reasoning. These manifestations spring from the realm of possibility, of potentiality, and no amount of analysis or computer algorithms will enable you to figure this out.

The good news is anyone can receive these kinds of communication. You do not need initials after your name or university credentials. You do not need to be rich or educated. You do not have to speak perfect English or English at all. It doesn't matter what color your skin is or how tall you are or if you are a man or a woman. It doesn't matter your religion, your culture, or the books you have read. It is your essence, the light radiating from within that guides you. Just as you have a heart and blood flows through your veins, you are designed as a spiritual, creative being, and no one is exempt.

Treat this as an opportunity to remember your very own experiences of connection to something beyond you. You must know this for yourself; experience the Essential Whisper for yourself, because no amount of fingers pointing to the moon makes the finger the moon. Synchronicities are the surest means we have for undisputedly getting information and direction. The significance of them, the "oh my God!" that accompanies these types of meaningful events, is your clue that you have just been whispered to.

~~~~~~~~~~~~~~~~~~~~~~~

Vitamin-Man, the man I met at Starbucks who told me about the "world's greatest vitamin" was an incredible synchronicity. I ended up bringing him home with me. After he told me about the vitamins, I remembered that I had overheard him talking to his friend at the next table about the law of attraction, so I asked, "Have you heard of the movie The Secret*?" He said that he heard about it twice in twenty-four hours! I told him, "I just borrowed it from a friend last night, and I was going to go home, literally go home and watch it this afternoon. Would you like to join me?"*

He followed me home to watch the movie. While I made him a turkey sandwich, he questioned me about being so trusting; after all, he was a stranger. He said he had the thought, This woman is really trusting.

Before then, I had never invited a stranger home. I told him, "I don't trust my ego, and this wasn't my ego. This was synchronistic, and I knew it was divine and benevolent."

While we sat talking, his mother called him on his cell phone, and he said to her, "Hey, Mom, guess what? I'm with my friend LaRue ... and, we're going to watch The Secret*". She told him, "Oh, son, I'm just about to watch* The Secret*."*

Can you see the pattern here? There is no way I could have planned or staged that series of events and made them meaningful and significant. As all of this was unfolding, deep inside me was the sense of peace and well-being. What I felt was the sensation of spaciousness that accompanies Whisper moments. There was a sense of no time and openness, and the sense of rightness to the events. I was being given what I had asked for and was simply following inner directions. I did not go to the coffee shop to engage in a discussion about vitamins or the law of attraction, but those subjects engaged me. They were there for me, and I could feel the sense and wonder of that.

~~~~~~~~~~~~~~~~~~~~

Dreams – Night Time Explorations

Each of us has a unique set of ways for receiving our messages—ways that are easiest for us to recognize and discern. Dreams can become a profound way to receive these messages. There are those who find it easy to receive communication from guidance through dreams. Perhaps this is true for you. Dreams allow the Whisper to speak without the mental distractions and the usual filters of perception. For many, though, dreams are usually symbolic in nature and are either not remembered upon waking or are difficult to interpret.

There are specific kinds of dreams of which you can more easily capture the meaning. Pay attention to those dreams that feel significant, are highly charged, are easy to remember, or that make you wonder about what they're telling you. Start there. If you already experience vivid and memorable dreams, begin to notice the messages and keep a dream journal. If you do not and would like to know what your dreams are telling you, then before you fall asleep, set the intention and desire for inner guidance to speak to you through your dreams and begin paying attention to whatever you remember and find significant.

~~~~~~~~~~~~~~~~~~~

I love going to bed at night! I call these "night time explorations," and I get teachings while I sleep. Often, I go to bed with a specific question for my Whisper, and I look forward to getting its response. I have discovered that I can ask, within the dream itself, what the meaning of the dream is, and then the symbolic nature of the dream is translated into words.

For me, these dreams, in which I am a participant, jumping from one scene to the next, are not linear in quality. These specific and significant dreams have a quality of an event taking place, as if on a movie screen, and I am the observer. In the dream, I am asking questions or wondering what is happening. The details of the dream are particularly clear, and I want to know what the dream means. There is a curiosity about it.

Here is one from my dream journal:

I am in the middle of Freeway I-635, north of Dallas to be exact, although not physically, with cars running over me; it is more like my presence is there. I notice this little green car. It's a funky little green car and small, European-looking. It's square like a box with two seats in the front and a little seat in the back. The doors in the back are like the sliding doors on a van. The dad is behind the wheel, and the mom is in the front seat, and this little girl is in the back seat, holding a doll. She looks to be five or six years old. I am watching this car coming toward me, and the mom and dad are zoned out as though they are in a trance. They have no awareness of what is going on in the back seat.

The back door slides open, and I'm thinking, Oh my God! And the little girl is holding the doll, standing it on the edge of the seat. The next thing I know, she throws the doll out in the middle of the traffic. The parents still don't have a clue; they are truly in a trance. This car is going fifty or sixty miles per hour, and I want to know what is going to happen next. Robotic and in a trance as well, the girl jumps out of the car, into the traffic.

I didn't recall anything after that, but I did ask for its meaning while still inside the dream. My soul said to me, "People are living unconsciously. You are here to awaken yourself and others from the trance of conditioning."

The dream showed me that my work is about awakening people from the trance of their conditioning.

The fact is, for many years, I lived the trance of conditioning. Conditioning numbs us. If you put a frog in a pot of boiling water, the frog jumps out. If you put a frog in room temperature water and slowly increase the heat, the frog will boil to death. That's what our conditioning does; it puts us in a trance like that, and it happens so gradually that we get used to it, and so, we become unconscious.

I got married at sixteen to escape my family and because I thought this man loved me, and I needed that. The abuse began with verbal put-downs. We both had affairs, and he was very hurt. The verbal abuse became intense and then escalated to physical abuse. At one point, while I was on the phone, he came in with a shotgun and he said, "I'm going to blow your fucking head off if you don't get off that phone!"

His face had veins sticking out, and I kind of giggled. The woman on the other end of the phone could hear the rage, and she hung up. She probably saved my life. One time he had choked me so hard that the blood vessels in my eyes were bloodshot. I didn't know this was abuse. He and I would watch the Phil Donahue show back in the seventies, when wife abuse started to become public. We would shake our heads and say, "Isn't that awful? How could someone do that to their mate like that? Isn't that just horrible?"

I was the frog in the room-temperature water, getting boiled to death. A friend plucked me out of the water and took me to a women's shelter. Divorce, to me, meant I would go to hell. I was already in hell, and I had already divorced him in my heart. So I got a legal divorce, because to my mind, I was going to hell anyway. I figured I might as well live it up while I'm on earth, and I did. I partied all night and worked all day, for a year. I dove in and out of depression, became ill, and wanted to end my life. I lived in a trance, and I understood the dream.

Dreams may reveal our deepest concerns, ambitions, and fears. They then go on to tell us what we need in order to change, grow, and evolve. If you are not getting these kinds of messages and would like to pay attention to your nighttime explorations, jump in and give it a try.

Direct Conversation – Talking to God

The voice of your Whisper is the group of distinct sensations that arise in you and direct your awareness of, and movement toward, an action or state of being. It was explained that the voice is not always a voice in the sense of an audible, verbal exchange that is heard with your ears. It is most often an impression or imprint in your being that is simultaneously translated for its meaning.

Your Whisper speaks to you through these experiences of presence. Certainly, you may have a direct or verbal kind of conversation, in which the sensations come with an internal interpretation given to you in words or direct impressions or even visual pictures. These words or impressions arise in the mind as thought, yet have the distinctive quality or sensation of neutrality and love.

A conversation with God is a flow with your Whisper, which would work something like this:

Whisper: You receive a distinct sensation from your Whisper, such as an Urge to take a certain action.

You: You respond by taking the action, going with the flow of the Urge, and following through with the action.

Whisper: You then meet someone who gives you just the right information, and it answers a question you had asked. Your Whisper is speaking to you through this individual.

You: You follow up on the information, and this becomes your response.

~~~~~~~~~~~~~~~~~~~~~~

I have watched countless people have direct communication with this wisdom for many years. I've watched client after client connect with this knowledge inside them and be brought to tears experiencing the profound peace that arises in the presence of truth.

One of the first of these was a minister. He said to me, "La Rue, I have been preaching every Sunday for thirty years, and if God answers prayer, God never answered my prayer." His wife was with him that day, and I told him that I wanted to teach him how to pray.

I told him, "Close your eyes and put your attention on your heart." I taught him what his attention was by placing his focus on his knee and then on his hand and on top of his head.

I said, "When you're praying you have questions, right? So what is it you want to know? Ask. Wait and breathe."

To this day, I don't know what he asked. He sat there in silence, pausing. The pause is so important. He opened his eyes, and he had his answer, and tears ran down his beautiful face—his dark, dark skin, so beautiful. The light made his tears look like diamonds running down his cheeks. He was so gorgeous, and I knew he had penetrated his heart. We sat there for another half hour while he prayed and got answers.

A few weeks later, he brought his whole church of thirty people to me, and I did a Saturday workshop for them and taught them how to pray. That was one of the most moving things I ever did in my life.

> **Every day becomes the practice of one continuous conversation and dialogue with this internal and ever-present guidance**

Most often, people become able and open to directly hear words from the Whisper when they ask an essential question. As discussed back in Chapter 5 on Wonderment, the *essential question* arises from a genuine desire to know the truth about what you are asking. It is the question that surfaces when the mind has exhausted all its possibilities, relinquished control, and finally said, "I don't know the answer to this, and I really want to know. Please tell me the answer."

The essential question is sometimes the down-and-out question, the one you truly want to know the answer to, from your heart. The reasoning mind is stilled; it has no more answers to offer. Essential questions come from the heart; they are heart-driven questions. The answers are the truth that resides inside you.

There's the story of a client who wanted to find out if she was pregnant. Muscle response feedback (kinesiology) can be used for this, because a body is either pregnant or not. Only one of these is true in any moment. When the question was posed and she was tested, the response was yes. She wanted to be tested again. This time, the response was no. Confused, she asked again, and the response was yes. She didn't want to be pregnant. She had a lot of stress around it and didn't want to know the truth. What she really wanted was some kind of assurance she wasn't pregnant.

Essential questions will spark a dialogue, an actual conversation, with your inner self. Any motive other than a desire for the truth blocks the truth and it is not heard, even as it is given. Through truth, miracles unfold and open up your life. The taste of these experiences, the delicious bounty of them, expands your heart with gratitude and awe. It becomes a conversation of gratitude.

I have a direct connect to my soul. The connection is free of static (unless I allow it). I'm empowered to hear my truth, feel my truth, and be my truth. I get the message from my soul much more clearly as to what my authentic self is, what the focus for my highest good is. I now have a friend who will always be with me, a friend that is a gift, a delight. That friend is my soul, my Whisper. My soul speaks to me. My soul just waits to play. More and more I experience life free of limiting beliefs, judgments, shame, and criticism. Instead, my life is filled with joy, acceptance, and much, much love and abundance. I recognize when something is amiss in my life, so I'm able to immediately address the hiccup, neutralize it, and move on."

Carol J. Q., Moncure, NC

Would You Like to Have a Conversation With God?

What is your essential question? What is it you *really* want to know? Please remember that essential questions are guided from the desire to know the truth. If you have one (or many), please write your question(s) here.

I *really* want to know … (Or you can ask, "What do *you* want me to know?") Write your question here:

Next: Close your eyes and deliberately place your attention and focus on your heart. Move your awareness to the area of your heart

Take several deep, long breaths, and when you feel relaxed and quiet, ask your essential question.

Wait.

Notice how your mind may want to jump in to answer it. Gently say, "Thank you," and ask the essential question again, from your heart.

Pause. Wait for the answer to arise or bubble up.

What is your answer? Write it here or in your journal.

Written and Spoken Words

If you believe that you fell into the world and that everything you see around you happens independently from you without your direct creative participation, then this means of interaction will seem a bit strange to you and outside of your paradigm.

The worldview you hold produces the world you see. The perceptions and beliefs about what you see hold your worldview in place. It is impossible to act outside of your belief system and pretend to believe something that you don't. Even if you try to pretend you believe something you don't, you are still acting from the belief of how you think you should be and how you want the world to see you, so hence the pretense. Most of the time, we are simply cruising along, acting and speaking from our beliefs, yet unaware of what our beliefs really are.

Miraculous and serendipitous situations seem to bypass your belief system; they kindle and ignite your sensibility and receptivity that something beyond what you can logically explain exists. A synchronous event cannot be explained logically; its cause and effect is unknown. Therefore, a flyer in the mail, for example, that answers a question that you have been wondering about or asking deeply about may be dismissed as a fluke or some kind of random chance, not related at all to your desire for an answer. As a result, these kinds of messages are ignored, shrugged off, disregarded, and considered inconsequential.

Synchronous events delight us, tickle us, and excite within us a knowing that we are creators on this journey. There is something very divine operating here, and when you get this, the world becomes your playground, and your soul your constant playmate. Pay attention to flyers in the mail, songs on the radio, and billboards when they deliver an answer to a wondering or question.

Dreams are one of the best ways for many to get messages from the Whisper. For others, flyers, songs, animals, and so on are the more common interactions.

～～～～～～～～～～～～～～～～～

From Vanessa; *I receive much of my direct information from written and spoken words. One day, I went to my kitchen pantry to make some beignets, which are a delicious and famous New Orleans doughnut. On this particular day, I had a craving for the treat, but discovered I had used the last box of mix. My husband had shipped home several boxes of the mix during a visit to New Orleans, but I knew of a store near my home that carried the product. When I got there, however, I couldn't find it, and the manager said he hadn't seen the mix in weeks. Disappointed and still desiring beignets, I resolved to locate the company online and wondered how to do that. The very next day, in the mail, was a full-color brochure from the exact beignet company in New Orleans, Café DuMonde! The brochure read, "We have five ways to order beignets."*

> **Consider this: when you receive answers to your questions, desires, and wonderings, you are giving yourself the answer. You are not separated from your intrinsic essence, so when you ask inside for an answer, you are asking that aspect of you, the wisdom of you that is connected to all that is. It is that facet of you that answers.**

Conversations – Everyone is Your Soul Mate

Have you ever run into someone you haven't seen in a while, and he gives you just the information you were looking for? You said to someone, "I was just thinking about that," or "That's exactly what I am looking for." Have you ever overheard a conversation about something you have been wondering about or asking for? Did you think these events were mere coincidences or did you wonder if they were something beyond coincidence?

Everything in front of you, the people, places, and events that are in your world, are there for you. It's all for you. There is pure goodness in this. When you have set clear intentions to be Whisper-directed, then you will notice more and more how the words from other people, whether spoken directly to you or just near you, can give you valuable information.

Everyone is your soul mate. Some people spend years, maybe a lifetime, searching for a soul mate, and what they miss is that everyone is connected to them. We see individual physical bodies and believe, "I'm over here and you're over there, so we must be separate." The invisible connection of the soul is not seen, but it is sensed.

Conversations become exciting as you wonder, "What will this person say that may help me to know what to do next?" Boredom is impossible from this vantage point. How can you become bored when the whole world has something for you? Begin to see every single thing occurring in your life as a gift to you from your soul and every person as your soul mate.

I decided to do some spring cleaning and throw out or give away items I didn't need or use. I came across several items I had kept in storage that belonged to an old friend of my son. I hadn't seen her in over a year, and I wondered what to do with her things. I remember thinking, Okay, God, if you want her to have her things, you had better find a way for her to show up.

A few days later, I went to my favorite Starbucks and came across a young man who was also a friend of my son since they were just boys. It was delightful to see him, and he asked me if I had heard of a book about the year 2012. This was the third time in just a few days that I had been given information about 2012, and my curiosity was piqued. I had already thought about getting this book. He reached into his backpack and handed me a book and told me I might find it interesting, I thought he just wanted me to see the book so I'd know which one to buy, but it became clear that he wanted me to keep it when he said, "Before I left the house, I had an urge to put this book in my backpack, and I didn't know why. Now I do. Please keep it and read it."

Then I had the thought to ask if he had seen the young woman whose belongings I still had. Amazingly, he said that he usually saw her two to three times a week!

~~~~~~~~~~~~~~~~~~~~~~

I refer to my new car as a gift from my Whisper. My former car was a 1995 Honda Passport and was twelve years old. Sure, it was a little beat up. The air-conditioning had given out a few years ago, and it had a wonderful designer windshield (another way to say a huge crack). I planned on waiting one more year before actively searching for a new car, for financial reasons. But my Whisper and the universe had other plans.

In March 2007, I attended a self-development class in Denton, Texas. One of my fun intentions was about getting a new car. I didn't really think that was possible. It was not a good idea financially, but after all, it was just an intention. After that, I found myself noticing cars, primarily Honda Pilots and Elements. I am a diehard Honda driver. But that was about it. I knew my money situation would not allow me that type of payment plan, and so I let go of the idea. Well, in late August of the same year, I decided I was going to take a trip to Michigan and walk the Mackinac Bridge. Every year, pedestrians are allowed to walk the five-mile suspension bridge on Labor Day. The Mighty Mac was celebrating its fiftieth year. It just so happened that my fiftieth birthday would follow a few months later. I decided to include a camping trip to the Upper Peninsula of Michigan and visit my family, as well. I was excited and ready for my adventure! One week before I was supposed to go, I took my car in for its checkup for the big trip. Later that day (Wednesday), my mechanic called to say that the only way I should take that car is if I was planning on walking back home to Arkansas. What was I going to do? I wondered.

I went home and decided not to worry about it. I would just let it go. I was going on my trip and had no idea how that was going to happen. The next day, I talked to a co-worker, who out of the blue, offered her car to take on my trip! Just like that!

I had an Urge to go car shopping that weekend before my trip, just to look. For the past few months, I had been doing research and gathering my credit scores. Little did I know those actions were getting me ready for this moment. I asked a male friend to go with me, and even though I cancelled due to rain, he convinced me to still go. What happened next was my Whisper in action.

We drove through the back car parking lot and never even made it to the front of the dealership. Down the last row of pre-owned vehicles, there it was. A 2007 Honda Fit. It was parked all by itself, new with fifty miles on it. My friend had been researching the Honda Fits and said the gas mileage and safety features were some of the best. I was skeptical, but as soon as I test-drove it, I knew. It was amazing—red with a manual transmission and enough room for camping equipment, plus it was fun to drive!

And to top it off, I had attracted the best car salesman ever in my days of purchasing cars. I have never had more fun buying a car in my life.

And so that night, I drove home in my new air-conditioned vehicle with affordable payments. Needless to say, I took my new car on my trip and had the time of my life. By living in the moment and listening to my Urges, wondering, and knowing, I am now driving a new car I didn't even know I wanted. My Whisper had planned more for me than I could have ever dreamed of for myself.

Sandy Staszkiewicz, Rogers, Arkansas

Symbols and Nature

For some people, certain numbers, colors, or animals show up often in their lives, and for them, these are significant events. Symbols can show up in our environment, nature, readings, and dreams.

These experiences happen quite often and are valid and distinct. As symbols present themselves to you, a Snapshot may occur, as well. The symbol's appearance is remembered as a vivid and clear experience that seems frozen in time and is meaningful to you. You may experience Collapsed Time when a meaningful symbol materializes in your world, during which the event takes on a surreal, slow-motion quality.

Be careful not to actively look and search for signs and symbols. This will cause you to engage analysis and attempt to give meaning to what you think is a symbol; you'll make up significance. People get into a bit of trouble with this when they interpret what they think the symbol means.

Please, don't spin imaginative stories around these events and try to figure out a symbol's meaning. Symbols are a way to give you information directly connected to an intention, a heartfelt desire, a wondering or an essential question. Symbols as well as the other interactive methods are always accompanied by one or more of the sensations of the Whisper, and the significance feels genuine, not conjured by wishful fantasy. You may not know the exact meaning or even the exact message, but there will be little doubt that you sense its significance.

For some people, symbols become the way their Whisper interacts most frequently or profoundly with them. Certain numbers, colors, or animals resonate and elicit recognition or importance.

From Vanessa: *While driving home late one evening, back in 1999, I glanced at the digital clock on the dashboard as it read 11:11, and a thought popped into my head out of the blue:* It must be my angels. *I don't know why I had that thought or how I made that connection. A few seconds later, Angela Winbush came on the radio, bellowing "Angel, angel." My heart raced so quickly that I had to pull my car over for a few minutes while I listened to the song.*

Since then, I see this symbol several times a day, regardless of what time it actually is. Just after daylight savings time in March 2008, none of the clocks in my house were set for the same time. One morning, the microwave oven clock showed 11:01, the clock on the oven showed 10:03, and as I moved to the coffeemaker to prepare my first cup of the day, the clock on the brewer displayed 11:11 PM!

For weeks after the initial event, however, I became increasingly agitated because I tried to figure out what the number meant. I looked it up and was astounded to find that thousands of people were also experiencing similar situations with this number. That only increased my need to figure this out. On one particular day, I saw that symbol several times throughout the day, and since 11:11 can only appear twice in a day, I became unnerved and shouted aloud that if it wasn't going to give me the meaning, it needed to stop! So it stopped. For three weeks, I saw no signs of that number or anything even resembling it.

Then an interesting thing happened: I noticed I missed it. I noticed that I had given myself fear over something that came in with such beauty and awe. And I noticed as I quietly reflected on that initial event that the meaning and the message came with the symbol: angels. My mental agitation was caused by trying to figure it out and make sense of it, asking myself over and over if it really meant angels.

For me now, it simply means angel, and when I see that number, as I continue to do sometimes several times a day, I am prompted to check inside to see what is being validated or what stream of thought I am running just then. It also reminds me to be grateful. There is such gratitude in the connection my soul made with me that night. Interestingly, that initial event occurred more than eight years ago, and I have not heard that song, by the woman who had an angel's name, on the radio since.

Finding Your Whisper Moments

Locating the Interactions

Can you find a time in your life when you were wondering about something or thinking about doing something, and soon after, you received a letter, a brochure, or a flyer that gave you just the information you were looking for?

Did you follow up on it or ignore it?

What happened after? Write your story here:

How does your Essential Whisper interact with you? Which way is the most comfortable for you or happens the most frequently (dreams, words, dialogue, symbols)?

Give yourself an example of one of the significant ways you heard from your Whisper. List all the ways you can find in your story of how the soul spoke to you. Writing this down gives you evidence that you have been spoken to all along and the distinct ways you receive this information. Spend some time with this!

~~~~~~~~~~~~~~~~~~~~~~~

The minister who said he had never gotten an answer to his prayers and then connected to the voice of God went in for surgery, gum cancer, and he died on the operating table.

Then he came back to life.

He told me when he left his body, he went up to the corner of the room and watched the doctors. He had an allergic reaction to the anesthesia, and he watched the heart monitor as it went … brppppp … flat line. He said he watched as they jabbed needles in him and put stuff into him to revive him, and he went … whfffff … back in the body.

He sat there with his wife as he told me this story. I had nicknames for them, Peepers and Kansey. Several years ago, I had written an article about them and this story. Kansey was upset with the hospital and doctors. She wanted to sue them. Peepers told her, "No, this isn't bad. It was a good thing." He said, "It was the highest spiritual experience I've ever had. I knew God!" It was so beautiful to listen to him, because he knew he wasn't his body, and he really lived knowing that. His wife Kansey died shortly after.

If we are praying and not getting answers, what are we praying to? Most people talk to their concept of God. You know, when we speak to a concept, a concept can't answer. A concept doesn't have an answer. But, when we speak to the source—if we don't define it as "something" and make it into something—then it is what it is without our definition, and it responds.

Peepers talked to God that day in his session when he placed his attention on his heart and asked his questions, and he got answers. He knew God answered prayer. He knew when he left his body that he wasn't his body. So, when his wife died, he knew she hadn't.

~~~~~~~~~~~~~~~~~~~~~~~

How does all this happen—synchronicities, dreams, and symbols giving us information? It seems a bit strange and outside the paradigm or worldview of most, right? Nothing clearly explains the phenomenon of our connection to all of it. It's all about the experience of this. The connection with divine goodness is a personal experience, not an intellectual exercise. Try it all on as an experiment, as self study. Let the experience of these interactions guide you; let the sensations lead the way. It's a practice you can embark on and become proficient in.

If you are not following your inner guidance, you will attempt to perceive meaning where there isn't any and look for signs and symbols. This is where it can get a bit tricky; remember, there are two voices: the mental voice and the Whisper's voice. Your job is to choose which of these you will follow. Ultimately, it is your only choice; it's the one decision to make.

The following chapter will ensure that you stay on course, listening to and following the distinct sensations of guidance and not the thoughts of ego. Knowing the differences will give you the certainty in this that you seek and now can have.

I was born as the fifth child in a family in poverty due to my father's alcoholism. I was the fourth girl, and from a very early age, I felt unwanted, both as another mouth to feed and a girl at that! I believed it would have been better for the family if I'd never been born. This severely affected my attitude toward life so much that I married an alcoholic, who sometimes became violent when drunk and was controlling when sober. I thought I could love him enough to help get him better.

In February 2005, I finally left my husband after thirty years of marriage. Around this time, my sister, an amazingly gifted and accredited journey therapist, offered me some journey therapy, which is like an intense internal personal journey. I was invited to go down some steps in my imagination, which helped me to let go of the thoughts usually swirling about my busy mind and allowed me to focus on becoming ready to listen. I pray regularly and am used to listening to God, who has spoken to me many times.

This particular day, I imagined that I was an egg in my mother's ovary. I know it sounds a bit weird, but it didn't feel weird at the time. There were lots of other eggs in there with me, but I was on the threshold and felt as though I was being jostled. I realized that they were all happy and smiling and acting as if it was a party. They were cheering for me, and I distinctly heard the words "Go on, it's your turn! Off you go!" The feelings I had overwhelmed me as I was so used to keeping my emotions in check in order to keep my marriage intact.

When I heard the eggs encouraging me, I felt very surprised. I'd never imagined before that I needed to be given permission to be happy to be alive! It was exhilarating and liberating, like seeing life through a brand-new color lens! It felt kind of strange, but it's something I am getting used to. After all, when you're learning to live with a new color, it takes time to weave it in to the rest of the strands of your life.

When I felt like a victim, I was terrified, flailing around, buffeted by every wind and storm that came along. Now I get in my boat, hold on to my Whisper, and enjoy the ride! When I become quiet, I ask, "What do you want me to learn from that one?" The answers are surprisingly gentler than the answers I would have given myself.

Today I know myself to be a fun-loving, decisive, powerful, beautiful, sensitive, compassionate, and intelligent woman, who, with the help of inner guidance, is putting myself first and seeing to my own needs.

Flo Perkins, Blackpool, UK

CHAPTER 15

※ Guidance vs. Disguise ※

Maneuvering Through the Noise of Thought

Now we come to the question that is asked most often, "How do I know I am listening to inner guidance and not to my ego's voice?" We are constantly bombarded with unceasing thoughts, and these thoughts just show up, all of the time. We feel them in our head, so we may believe they originate there. One day, you may notice that you don't seem to have very much to do with it. This is the way it is with thoughts. For a few moments, stop reading, sit, and notice the thoughts that float in.

Are you able to get a glimpse of how they simply arrive with no real rhyme or reason to them? Of course, there are those thoughts that stick around for a while; they seem to hang out in your head as if crying out for a bit of attention. If you try to push them away, they come back. You may have noticed that some have a different tone than others. Remember when LaRue was following the SanderMan back to his house, and she heard her mother's voice yelling in her head, "What are you doing? He is a stranger!"? Thoughts seem to have personality. They have taken on the personality of the voice from which they originated, the persona of the individual we believed: our parent, our teacher, our peers, and so forth.

Thoughts come in all manner of flavors and qualities, such as thoughts of argument, thoughts of reason, thoughts of conviction, thoughts of denial, thoughts of aggression or revenge, thoughts of love, thoughts of kindness, thoughts of what to do, thoughts of how to be, thoughts of who is right or wrong, thoughts of war, thoughts of work, thoughts of the past, thoughts of the future, thoughts of worry, thoughts of people, places, and things.

No wonder we can hardly hear our Essential Whisper! Is it any wonder we find it difficult to distinguish this incessant stream of thoughts from the truth of our essence? Hopefully, this chapter will, once and for all, help you to know the difference between streams of thought and the voice of inner guidance. You will still have to practice this for a while at least, given thoughts whip in quite quickly and often under the radar, but you will know exactly what to practice.

Will the Real Voice Please Stand Up?

Back in the late sixties, there was a television game show, *To Tell the Truth*. It was a classic game show, in which a person of some notoriety and two impostors try to match wits with a panel of four celebrities. The object of the game was to try to fool the celebrities into voting for the two impostors.

It is a bit like that when determining the voice of guidance from the voice of disguise, which does a pretty good job fooling us into believing it's the Whisper, but only until you know the real deal. By now, you've become very familiar with the distinct sensations, and the Six Distinct Experiences. At the end of the book is an eight-week guide that will lead you even deeper into your experiences with your Whisper.

There are feelings and thoughts that seem to mimic the energy and sensations of inner guidance and can seem as if they are the real deal. So let us look at Snapshot-Click, Collapsed Time, Urge, Wonderment, Knowing, and Inspiration in the chart below and compare these distinctive and distinguishable qualities to the mental characteristics that may fool you into believing that you have heard from inner guidance, the sensations of the Whisper.

Mental Characteristic	Your Essential Whisper
Memory—Recollection	**Snapshot-Click**
Recollection occurs when recalling a memory that you are consciously bringing back to mind, often with some effort. In this case, we spin stories around the memory, making them mean something.	When you have a snapshot, the memory surfaces without any effort and has a great sense of significance. When you recognize the significance, it feels like the realization clicked into place. The Click tells you the meaning.

Time	Collapsed Time
Time is a continuum, measured in terms of events, which succeed one another from past, through present, to future. There is the perception of time as a continuum of one event, to the next event, to the next event.	This is a sudden loss of the sense of a continuum or the value or effect of time. Time seems to break down suddenly and give way to "no time," when events seem to happen all at once.
Emergency	**Urge**
An emergency is an unforeseen combination of circumstances or the resulting state that calls for immediate action. It's an urgent need for assistance or relief. It's a juncture that is a point of time, especially one made critical by a concurrence of circumstances.	A continuing impulse toward an activity or goal. To undertake the accomplishment of something with energy, swiftness, or enthusiasm. With an urge emanating from soul, there is energy to move toward a goal or action, often without reason or knowing why.
Analysis	**Wonderment**
Analysis is the separation of the whole into its component parts. It's an examination of a complex, its elements, and their relationships. To analyze means to study or determine the nature and relationship of the part by analysis	When you only have a part of an idea or reason and are looking for the whole, you are wondering. You are in a state of rapt attention or astonishment at something awesomely mysterious or new to your experience. This is effective or efficient far beyond anything previously known or anticipated. Essential means "of, relating to, or constituting essence; of the utmost importance." The essential question is the act of asking an important question that looks to seek an experience of one's essence.
Believing	**Knowing**
To accept as true, genuine, or real. To hold an opinion or to think. To consider to be true or honest and to accept the word or evidence of.	Knowing is to be shrewdly and keenly alert to the possession of exclusive inside knowledge or information. It's the condition of being aware of something, of being cognizant—to re cognize or to know again.

Mania	Inspiration
Mania is wild or violent thinking; to be obsessive about something. It is excitement, manifested by mental and physical hyperactivity, disorganization of behavior, and an elevation of mood, with unreasonable enthusiasm.	Inspiration is a stimulus to creative thought. It means to stimulate or impel to some creative effort or to motivate as by divine influence. To be inspired is to be energized by the motivation to create; encouraged.

Did you discern the differences between the mental characteristics and the qualities of your Essential Whisper? Positioned side by side, you can readily see the distinctions.

That chart shows you the comparison between of the qualities of the mental characteristics and the sensations. Next is the chart that will show you the specific thoughts that are associated with experiences of particular emotional or mental states compared to states of being. Remember, thoughts (or beliefs) and their associated feelings are attached. This is why once you connect to the sensations of the Whisper's voice, which are spaciousness, energy, peace, joy, stillness, certainty, and presence, you will notice that the thoughts or the messages that are connected will align with those deep sensations; they'll resonate.

What is the difference between what we say to ourselves when we are listening to mental thoughts and what we say to ourselves when we are listening to the Whisper? This is the key to really knowing, with absolute certainty, when you are listening to the Whisper or not.

There are specific thoughts that emanate from the ego (belief system) and not from your Whisper. These thoughts feel very true, because they are tied to beliefs. Freezing them on paper for you to look at on the page puts them into perspective. Typed and static, they are not swirling around in your head but instead frozen right here in black and white for you to look at and recognize. Compare the voice of disguise to the thoughts of guidance and notice which ones you recognize.

The Voice of Disguise	The Voice of Guidance
Recollection	**Snapshot-Click**
These are memories of painful, sad, or strongly emotional events, in which you tell stories around the memory, and which fluctuate and change; there is effort to recall the memory.	This is a stilled moment in time when the event is frozen and stands out clearly and is detailed like a camera photo. The memory surfaces and is highly significant and meaningful but not emotional.
• I was abused, hurt, raped, etc. • I remember this, and then this, and then this. • It was all so confusing. • It happened so fast, I was shocked. • It was the happiest time in my life. • I hated it when … • That was the best time in my life. • I was itching all over. • I couldn't breathe.	• When I was hurt there was a moment when I looked into his eyes; it was so clear. • In that moment, everything else faded and only this stands out. • The details are so clear and the colors stand out. • The moment stopped, and there was this peace inside me. I felt such love. • Even though I was itching all over, I heard "Stop," and in that moment, all the itching went away; I stared at my leg and it was so clear and I noticed …
Time	**Collapsed Time and Space**
Time is felt as concrete and limited. Memories involving time have a beginning and end and are	The sense of time feels expanded, even non-existent. Space is fluid.
• There wasn't enough time. • There isn't enough time. • I had to make a decision quickly. • I was rushed into doing … • I had a deadline; that's why I did that.	• It seemed like I had all the time in the world. • All of a sudden, time stopped. • What should have taken months took only moments. • Time seemed to stretch.

• We should plan for the future. • There's no time like the present. • You have only three months to live. • I've wasted so much time. • I have so much to do. • I'll never get it all done.	• There is no decision to make. • Life unfolds perfectly. • Everyone dies on time. • I felt this openness, like time (space) expanded. • Even though it happened so fast, I felt such peace and presence.

Emergency	**Urge**
If you find yourself in an emergency in which a circumstance requires your immediate attention and the situation is critical, take a moment to go inside and ask your soul to guide you and then take action. These examples below are when you think you are urged by the soul, but in fact you believe it is an emergency.	The soul urges by infusing your being with energy to take a particular action, and you don't know why at that moment. Trying to figure out why engages the thinking mind, which has to figure it out but cannot access infinite possibilities.
• I had to move fast. • There was no time to waste. • I was urged to call and give her the truth. • I knew I had to go because it would be wrong not to. • It felt important to be there because … • She needed to hear the truth, because what she was doing was a mistake. • I had to make that trip because his feelings would have been hurt. • I had to because … • I need to because … • I am compelled to because …	• I had this strong feeling to move. • I was energized to do this. • It was weird. I just felt to call her. • I had this sense to go and be there. • I just followed my energy to be there. • I had no idea what I was going to say; I just felt an urge to call her. • It was like I felt called to make that trip and be there. • I wasn't sure his feelings might be hurt, but I simply had no urge from my soul to make that trip, even though he wanted me to. • I didn't go. I simply wasn't moved to go. • I didn't need anything at the store, but I felt an urge to go anyway.

Analysis	Wonderment
As soon as you say "because," you are giving reasons for your beliefs. There is nothing wrong with analysis, just don't confuse it with the voice of your heart.	Wonderment is the complete surprise and amazement that what you have asked, what you are seeking, has shown up in this remarkable, delightful way.

<table>
<tr><td>

- I had to because …
- I need to because …
- It's right because …
- I know it because …
- These are the reasons …
- This is how it is done …
- This is how it has always been done …
- There is no other way …
- I've exhausted all the possibilities …
- My soul told me to do this because …
- It can't (won't, doesn't, shouldn't, wouldn't) happen without (with) …
- I was directed by my soul because …
- I thought it through, and my soul said …
- I know it was my soul because it just made sense.
- This just has to work.

</td><td>

- I got the world's best vitamins right there at Starbucks!
- And then there it was right before my eyes.
- It's like a miracle.
- I would have never thought it could happen like this.
- Wow!
- Oh my God!
- She just showed up.
- There it was, the answer to my question.
- I would never have thought it could happen that way.
- That's amazing the way that happened.
- I felt so good when that occurred like that.
- No way could I have planned that.
- It turned out better than I could have imagined.
- It was the perfect answer to my question.

</td></tr>
</table>

Believing	Knowing
With a belief, you accept something as true; you have supporting evidence and experience that proves it, and you feel it as true.	Knowing gives you no basis for truth. It feels like cellular alignment in your whole being, so you just know to do something, and there is great peace in it. And although it has never occurred to you to do this, you recognize it. Knowing is for you; you cannot know for someone else.
<ul><li>I have to have the surgery.</li><li>I don't know another way.</li><li>There is no other way.</li><li>I don't know what I want.</li><li>I have to prove myself.</li><li>I don't know what to do.</li><li>I don't know what this person or situation is showing me.</li><li>It will never happen.</li><li>I am mentally blocked.</li><li>How can anyone know this?</li><li>It's impossible.</li><li>I know my soul told me to do this because …</li><li>It felt like the right thing to do because …</li><li>It has to be the right thing to do.</li><li>I am right.</li><li>I know not to follow you because you are wrong.</li><li>There is only one right way to do this.</li><li>I know the answer my soul told me.</li><li>I know what she should do.</li><li>I know it in my bones what he should do.</li><li>There's no question that he is doing it right (wrong).</li></ul>	<ul><li>All of a sudden, I just knew it would be okay.</li><li>I just knew to have the surgery, and all the fear went away.</li><li>I had no idea how I knew; I just did.</li><li>As soon as I heard those words, I knew to do that.</li><li>It was like my whole body vibrated with that knowing.</li><li>Everything told me differently, but I simply knew to do it this way.</li><li>It was like the cells lined up in my body, and I knew.</li><li>Everybody was telling me differently, but somehow I just knew.</li><li>This feeling of knowing happened quickly; it was surprising.</li><li>I simply couldn't be talked out of it, but I had no idea how I knew.</li><li>Once I acted on the knowing, it seemed the doors to the universe flung open; it was so easy.</li><li>I didn't have to defend the knowing; I felt no urge to argue that I knew.</li></ul>

Mania	Inspiration
Mania is often confused with inspiration, as there is this high excitement that mimics the high energy of inspiration. Mania has an obsessive thinking and behavior to it, and a false energy, stimulated by intense excitement. This one, most of all, is confused with the soul's gentle guidance to create. There is an addictive quality to mania; the high excitement is emotionally addictive, and when it burns out, it drops to feelings of depression and depletion. Mania is distinguishable in that there is an anticipated result or outcome that is motivating the excitement. This is not psychology; this is thinking in action. We must respond to our beliefs, and our bodies also must respond.	Inspiration literally means to breathe in, to "in-spirit" or to be infused with spirit. It is energy to create. We are creators with the divine and are given particular talents and skills to create using our unique blueprint. When infused with this energy, great love and desire to take action occur. You are excited, but not obsessively or exceedingly so. You are excited to see what will be created. Not following Inspiration will result in an energy drop, which will feel like depression, tiredness, and fatigue.
• When I do this I will make a ton of money! • You must do this with me. It will be so fun. • I can't wait to get started, just think of all that will happen… • Once I do this, I'll never have to worry again! • Isn't this so amazing it fell in my lap and I knew I had to do this because when it is done I'll be able to … • I've been thinking about this for years and now I am so excited because the time is right and I just know when I accomplish this I will be able to …	• I felt this high energy to create this. • I have this idea. Does this interest you? • This poetry just started writing itself in my head and wouldn't stop until I finally got up and wrote it down. There were profound messages for me in the poems. • I felt this high energy to create this. • I have this idea. Does this interest you?

- Can you believe how this just fell in my lap it must be divine because ...
- I know it is God telling me to do this because I have wanted to for so long and now look how it is turning out and I just can't wait to get started because my whole life is going to change and you should do this too.
- They told me I was just the right person to do this and I am so excited it is the perfect job for me and all I have to do now is get some training but that is no big deal because they are going to give that to me and anyway the money is so good I will be able to get that car I had my eye on and this is just what I wanted to do, it's much better than what I am doing now this job sucks and now I will be able to ...
- Oh my God he is the perfect man for me he even told me my secret phrase how good is that and then when we argued the way he made up was so sensitive. I am so happy my life will be so different with him in it. I can't stop thinking about him I'm going to call him right now, you know, just to check in.

- This poetry just started writing itself in my head and wouldn't stop until I finally got up and wrote it down. There were profound messages for me in the poems.
- People would ask me to teach, so I did, and when I noticed how their lives changed, I was inspired to develop more courses. I had no idea how to do this, but I just followed the energy, and the information came through.
- I wanted to paint my little chest and knew to do it within those four days; it was so much fun to paint it, and I even got to meet SanderMan to boot.
- I sat down to watch TV, but the remote flew out of my hand as if it was knocked out. So I became quiet and went inside. This flurry of affirmations came to me, and I had to jump up and write them down.
- In the shower, I heard the words "SoulTalk Café" and with it, images of a café setting, like a French bistro with tables and chairs. I was so energized to create that environment, and we had the most attractive booth. People just flocked to us; many of our future students came that day.
- I was thinking about how people block receiving what they desire and just don't recognize it, and suddenly this surge of energy rushed through me, and I wrote the course "Receiving Your Heart's Desire" in just a few hours.

	• I knew I wanted to write a book, so, I tried to, but the energy for it wasn't there. So I asked my soul to help me. Now this book is being written, and essential questions have inspired it. We are creating courses, supplements, and games to go with it, and the energy is just inspiring all kinds of neat ideas… • One day I was energized to paint my office and I did, and now it is such a soothing color to work in.

Can you see the differences in the thoughts and beliefs in both columns? Did you notice the difference in the language in the above examples? It takes practice to catch yourself having specific thoughts, freeze them, and to notice how you convince yourself of their truth. Remember this: go in first, to the place where you connect to your sensations, and ask guidance for the truth.

Thoughts fly into your mind very rapidly. Do not become discouraged; you are exercising the muscle of conscious awareness. You are enlightening yourself. It won't take long at all. Review these charts often; they will help you to maneuver through the noise of thought.

Well, you are almost there! Are you better able to recognize, trust, and follow inner guidance, your Whisper, with absolute certainty? Certainty is critical here. Without it, you are right back to where you started: guessing. The guesswork has been removed. You've found experiences of the Six Distinct Ways and how the sensations of inner guidance show up and can be recognized. You've discovered the ways you are guided through various interactions such as dreams, symbols, and synchronicities.

And, most important, you've maneuvered through the noise of thought and the other voices in your head. Just to be sure you have a way to go deeper and give yourself more experiences, there is the eight-week guide at the end that you can take yourself through at your own pace. You'll find supplementary audios at http://www.ILoveMyWhisper.com. So, what's left?

Have you sensed the divineness of it yet? Does it feel joyful?

It's not enough to have certainty in your life if you miss the joy. It's not enough to develop a partnership with your Whisper if you miss the divine goodness of it all. Then it's nothing more than a pleasant exercise and an intellectual pursuit. Although that's okay, why not give you all of it?

In the final chapter, the final journey, you are introduced to joy. With peace comes joy. They hold hands, they walk arm in arm, side by side. Peace and joy—like peanut butter and jelly.

CHAPTER 16

❧ Your Essential Nature ❦

Embracing Inner Joy

You may recall when the national news was filled with stories of the shooting incident that took place at Virginia Tech.

A student of the school shot over thirty students and faculty, and then himself. Tragedies of this magnitude often leave us dazed, wondering how something like this can occur. Another question might be, "Where was God?" Was this student following his Whisper? Was his soul leading him to commit these acts against himself and others?

A Course in Miracles states "No one can organize his life without some thought system. Once you have developed a thought system of any kind, you live by it and teach it."

We have to respond from, or act out of, our belief system. We can choose what to believe, or at least look at our beliefs. We can choose to change what we believe, as we notice which beliefs bring us stress. But we cannot choose to act outside of our beliefs. Our beliefs and our actions are one and the same. The free will we have allows us to take a look at each belief and ask, "How does it feel to have this belief?" We are given distinct sensations all along the way that alert us when we are aligned with, or when we have moved away from, our inherent nature of peace. When we have moved away from peace, it hurts; we feel this as stress and discomfort.

A disconnected heart, one separated from peace, hurts. This student was confused. A confused mind with confused thinking precipitates confused actions.

Connecting our heart to peace—who teaches this? What classroom do we get this in? Growing up, weren't you told to ignore feelings and think through to the answer? Recognizing and following your Whisper is as easy as brushing your teeth, once you know and have connected to the sensations. Experiencing your Essential Whisper and living from the voice of your soul—your essential nature—is one way to be the teacher of this, the classroom.

> **We are destined, it seems, to act out our beliefs, until we don't believe them anymore, and perhaps to experience everything that moves us from love, until we come to understand that nothing can move us from love.**

How do we know which of our beliefs need to be changed or looked at? We can take another look at the beliefs we hold that bring stress or pain.

I have come to experience that I can be ill, sick in bed, and still have a happy life. I no longer hold the belief that I have to suffer just because my body is experiencing a change. Before, I would suffer in my mind, as well as in my body! I would lie in bed and think, Why am I sick? I have too many things to do! I can't be sick today. I don't want to be sick. *I would think these thoughts and believe them and cause all kinds of suffering. Now, when this body gets ill, I climb into bed and bask in the illness. I fully feel all the aches or tiredness. If I am moved to go to the doctor, I go. I do what the doctor tells me, and I immerse myself in the body's response to what it needs in each moment. This is what I mean when I say I can have a happy life while being sick. The body is sick, but my mind is free to fully be in the experience.*

What would someone such as this student, the shooter at the college, have to believe in order to act out from pain and suffering? He simply didn't have a way to ask if any of it was true. He had no choice, without deep inquiry of his beliefs, but to believe them.

This is not the voice of divine guidance, which simply waits for you to ask and then lovingly responds through the inner sensations of neutrality, peace, and expansion. Loud, incessant thoughts of hatred, shame, and guilt block the awareness of the internal Whisper. That's why we have given you many ways to find your Whisper within and to connect to the distinct sensations of its voice, rather than to the feelings and symptoms of resistance.

And yet, even in all this seeming chaos and insanity, there is a divine perfection unlike anything we can imagine as perfect or judge as divine. In your quiet moments, you will find some remarkable experiences that have shown you that love is the reigning power and has never left your side. How could it?

You Are Designed For Joy

You are designed for joy. Does this sound like the truth to you? It may not if you are not experiencing joy in your life. It may seem unattainable, a dream for dreamers. Life is filled with pain and suffering, it can be argued, and there is certainly enough evidence that this is true.

Our inherent nature, our essence of peace and its byproduct, joy, is as natural to us as breathing. It is only when we move away from our nature, by believing stressful and painful thoughts, that we feel the ache. The pain stabs us, and the suffering simmers inside us whenever we fight or resist the natural tendency for joy. As you consider how and when the Six Distinct Experiences have shown up in your life, notice the sensations. Notice the peace you felt. Notice the contentment that swept you. Notice in Wonderment the joy of the amazement and awe. Notice in Collapsed Time the taste of eternity you experienced. Notice how synchronicities surprised and delighted you. In all of this, notice the joy of life. Can you sense the wondrous flow of it all?

So, what do we do when we become confused by the all the information the world hands us or when stress overcomes joy, making it hard to hear our Essential Whisper? How can we find joy then?

~~~~~~~~~~~~~~~~~~~

I certainly know that back when I was suicidal, really struggling financially and socially, pretending to be what I wasn't, no one could have told me I was designed for joy. Joy was something I ached for, but I didn't know how to experience it. The ache was my message that I was not living according to my inherent or intrinsic nature. But how could I know that then?

One day, while facilitating a class in Austin, Texas, I found myself spontaneously sharing a memory of when I was an infant. I may have been six or seven months old. Until that moment, I had no prior plan to share this memory, and until I spoke it out loud, I never knew the power of its significance in my life. Yet I had remembered it my entire life. The class was mesmerized as I told the story. Interestingly, this story, this memory, was flowing out of me, as if it were happening right then. Somehow, as

I shared this early memory, the telling of it fired up my neurology in such a way that it was alive in me, so vivid and so real.

Fortunately, it was being recorded, so now I can share it. My sister, eleven years my elder, and I were in the one and only bathroom in our home. We had one of those sinks that hung on the wall with the plumbing showing below. Above the sink, there was a standard white metal medicine cabinet with a mirrored door. My sister stood me up in front of the mirror, with my little feet perched on the cold porcelain sink. She lifted me up and pointed to me in the mirror. When I looked, I could see her there, and I could see a small, little body there, too. She pointed to the small body, and with so much excitement in her voice, said, "Look! That is you!" I looked into my big, blue, baby eyes and felt, "Wow!" I felt such inexpressible joy! Joy to be me! It was at that moment I became separate and distinct from the background, which up until then, I had been one with. This was my glorious introduction to separation.

My family lovingly began teaching me words and labels for things. I will never forget when my sweet sister pointed to a flower and said, "Fl ow er," and the flower stood out from the background. I could see color and shape. I could see it there, although I didn't have a name or label for it then. Later, it became known as a red petunia.

At first, the flower was just one with everything else. As she said the word "fl ow er" and taught me to say flower, the object became a flower. The flower popped out from the background, and it became something—something that was distinguishable from the rest of the background. In the separation of the flower from its background, there was an immense joy inside me. I realized, in the telling of this memory, that there was a real joy in separation. It was amazing how I remembered that time in my life, when I was just a toddler.

I asked the class if they remembered when they first had the concept of a self, if they remembered the moment that they perceived themselves as being separate from the background, separate from the whole. There was stillness in the room. No sounds. No movement. There was only peaceful, clear silence. No one remembered having this kind of experience. I was intrigued to realize that I was alone in this memory of separation. At some point, someone responded, "No, I don't remember the moment I had a concept of myself for the first time, but your description of it makes it real for me. It is as though your concept, your reality, was one-dimensional, and when your family brought these things out, life became three dimensional."

When my sister introduced me to myself, I felt the elation of "Meeee! I am a meee!" Being introduced to a flower was such a joyful experience, and now I am feeling the same elation as I drop a concept or a label or a belief. As the world, for me, begins to fall back into oneness, I feel that same joy. As I begin to lose my sense of self, these things that were once separate—cups or trees or flowers—are now part of the whole again; merging into oneness is just as joyful!

We separate self, and we come back, and it is all joyful.

It's all joyful. Yet it wasn't until I told the story and relived the memory, right there in front of the class, that I knew the journey into separation was so very exciting and so very joyful.

I can't speak for the others, but I felt the presence of love in the room. There was a palpable pulsation, as if I were in the heartbeat of God. Even now, the experience has remained and intensified. That day, I had touched the full presence of God. A few days later, I awakened in the early morning hours with the words, "the Final Journey."

The Final Journey is the journey to a place of peace that resides within. You don't have to die a physical death to go to heaven. Heaven exists within you, right here, right now.

So ultimately, we cannot know what was passing through the mind of the Virginia Tech student. We cannot know the deep pain he felt and experienced, nor can we know, in the end, what this shooting was all for. What experience teaches is that everything teaches. Everything is love. Love was not created, and love cannot be destroyed. There was never a time when love did not exist, and there will never be a time when love will not exist. Love IS. Byron Katie once said, "God is good, God is everything, and that is the final story."

What we have been given—perhaps by design, perhaps by grace—is a distinct roadmap on this journey, a compass that points the way. No one has to wander the terrain following breadcrumbs. There is a clear path, with guideposts set out all along the way. The journey begins and ends with you.

SECTION FOUR

Creating a Partnership with
Your Whisper

An Eight-Week Practice Guide and Journal

Creating a Partnership with Your Whisper

During the next eight weeks, you will connect with certainty to your Essential Whisper, which has spoken all along but perhaps was not always recognized as your higher wisdom. Now that you know what the distinctive sensations of this energy are, you can develop your own personal practice. Your individualized intrinsic print is designed such that you have your own ways to express your values, talents, and gifts. This is what makes your practice unique to you.

This eight-week practice guide is just that, a guide. When it comes to hearing your Essential Whisper, there are no hard and fast rules. Use the guide the way you are moved to. How you use this practice is the practice of following intuitive guidance. Please release any of the *shoulds* or guilt about the right way to do this.

Here is what you need to know about how this guide was designed for you. Dividing a practice into chunks is easiest for most people, so this guide is divided into eight chunks or sections, which you can do weekly for eight weeks.

Weeks 1–6 help you to increase your confidence in recognizing, trusting, and following the sensations, along with each of the six experiences.

Weeks 7–8 help you to create your unique and distinctive practice using the method by which you receive your messages and utilizing your intrinsic values and design.

There are *free* audio supplements for each of the eight sections or weeks. Visit http://www.ILoveMyWhisper.com and click "audio lessons."

Your Weekly Schedule

Each day you will do the simple Anchoring Meditation (Appendix A) as early as you can after you awaken. This will help you quiet your mind and set your intention. You will choose to listen to your Whisper that day. Then at some point during the week, you can spend thirty minutes to an hour locating the times in your life when you've experienced Snapshot-Click, Collapsed Time, Urge, Wonderment, Knowing, and Inspiration. Throughout the week, as you get information from your guidance or have memories pop up for you, write them in your journal or notebook.

Each week, to help you *become a master* at dialoguing with your Whisper, you will have a practice assignment. These assignments will be fun and playful and will take as long as you want to take with them, although they are designed to be completed within a couple of hours.

Developing a partnership with the soul is a lighthearted way to experience peace and joy. There is nothing serious about partnering with yourself except having a serious willingness to choose to develop this intimate relationship.

What You Need

- Two to four hours per week of uninterrupted time. This does not have to be continuous time. Please feel free to spread this out during the week as convenient. There are basically four activities for each practice session: Anchoring Meditation, locating the distinctive quality for that week, completing the practice exercise, and recording your experiences.

- A journal or notebook to capture your stories, memories, experiences of guidance, impressions, synchronicities, dreams, and so forth. This is a must! You are capturing in your journal the subtle and not so subtle ways you dialogue with your soul. Keeping an ongoing record is invaluable as you continue fine-tuning your moment to moment partnership. If you would like to download a complimentary journal for the Essential Whisper practice please go to http://www.ILoveMyWhisper.com and click on "The Essential Guide Journal."

You can then three-hole-punch this journal and place it in a three-ring binder.

- A practice buddy (optional). Doing this practice with a partner can be such fun. With a practice buddy, you can share your results and successes communicating with your creating self. You can share your doubts and questions, as well. You can encourage each other and be a sounding board for one another.

Please feel free to start a group to practice together. We only ask that you remain within the integrity of this book and follow the practice guide for the *sole* purpose of honoring your inherent nature of love and peace. Also, if you are interested in a guided class, we offer Whisper tele-seminars and an Inner Advantage tele-course, where you can join us as we guide you through a six-week comprehensive program.

To get more information, please visit
http://www.InnerAdvantageTraining.com.

Your Weekly Summary

Each week for eight weeks you will:

- Read the Distinct Experience Description and read or reread the corresponding chapter if necessary.
- Review the Essential Lesson. This will give you an additional lesson in understanding the specific experience you are focusing on that week
- Do the Daily Anchoring Meditation and select which channel you will use that day: intention, choosing, attention, or noticing. You may want to determine what essential question or wondering you would like your Whisper to answer for you. This is a quiet time to reflect on your life and pull up memories of when you experienced one (or more) of the distinctive sensations or experiences.
- Complete the practice assignment. Record in your journal your dialogue with guidance and what happens in your life as you act on or follow through with your messages.
- Go online to listen to the weekly audio explanation and supplement. Go to http://www.ILoveMyWhisper.com.

That's it! Here are just some of the benefits recognizing, trusting, and following your Essential Whisper will bring you.

- You will be aided in producing desired results in your life because you will stop going against your natural life print.

- You will recognize nonverbal intuitive messages with trust and certainty; no more second-guessing yourself!

- You will live with a greater sense of ease in your life because you know you have within you a perfect and divine guidance system to help you make decisions

- You will experience more energy; you will no longer resist your inner guidance and spend energy doing things that don't align with your highest values.

- You will become intimate with the sensations of inner guidance and know when it is your personality self or your soul whispering to you.

- You will have more peace in your life as you uncover the beliefs that cause discomfort and stress.

Are you ready to get started?
Let us take this *journey* together!

Week 1: Snapshot-Click

If you haven't read Chapter 2 - Snapshot-Click, please return to that chapter and read it before *doing this exercise*

The Distinct Experience

A Snapshot-Click is a moment in your life that stands out as highly meaningful and significant to you and is stilled in your mind like a photograph. The significance, when it becomes known to you, feels like a click of recognition; the memory is clear and distinct, and the meaning is relevant in your life. Connecting these snapshot moments in your life reveals a divine story or message to you, like connecting the pieces of a puzzle reveals the whole picture.

The Essential Lesson

These distinctive qualities are experiences of grace. Grace is the embodiment of love given or shown to us without our having to do anything to receive it. Snapshots are memories of the truth of love.

Locating Snap Click

Do the Anchoring Meditation (Appendix A) and select a specific channel (Chapter 10) you will use to tune into the Whisper (attention, intention, choosing, noticing).

This week I will use _____to tune in.
(Noticing, Conscious choice, Intention, Attention)

My essential-question or wondering this week is:

_____

On the following pages, you will see a diagram of a golden thread connecting photograph frames. As you recall a Snapshot moment, write your story within the frame. Then, above or below the frame, write what the significance of the memory is to you … what clicks. This week find at least three Snapshot-Clicks. Be as detailed as you can.

- What are the sensations you recall in the Snapshot-Click?
- Does the Snapshot (memory) have any of the other distinctive qualities to it?

This Week's Practice

This week, please *notice* the frames in your life as you go about your daily activities. As you bring awareness to Snapshot-Click, you may begin to see your life lived frame by frame by frame. Each moment is significant; nothing is wasted. What stands out this week? Connect the golden thread.

Remember to visit http://www.ILoveMyWhisper.com and click on "Audio Lesson Week 1."

The Golden Thread

The Golden Thread

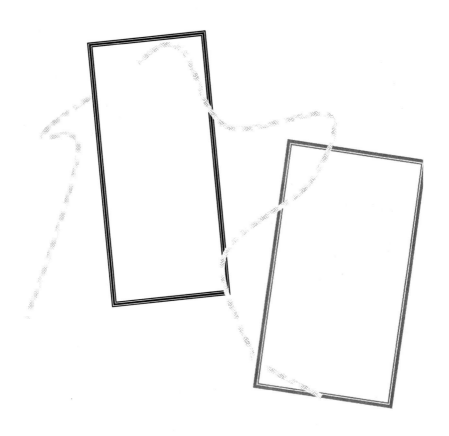

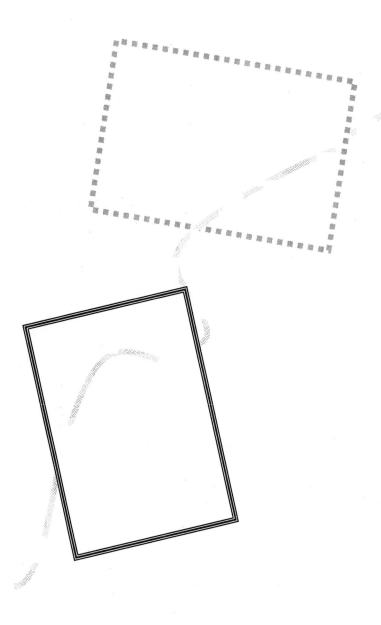

Week 2: Collapsed Time and Space

If you haven't read Chapter 3, Collapsed Time and Space, please return to that chapter and read it **before** *doing these exercises.*

The Distinct Experience
Time and space are perceived as a continuum. Time exists as the perception of events in sequence, and space as that which we move through. Collapsed Time and Space as a Distinct Experience changes the rules we have about time and space. This event feels timeless and eternal. You've called these events miracles.

The Essential Lesson
You have a strong sense of heightened presence, the eternal, the now. You hear your divine messages clearest when the mind is still. These experiences move you closer to understanding you are eternal, and in presence, your essence is peace. Your Essential Whisper speaks very clearly in these moments. Have you wondered whose timing we're really on?

Locating Collapsed Time and Space
Do the Anchoring Meditation (Appendix A) and select a specific channel to use to tune into the Whisper.

This week I will use _____ to tune in.
(Noticing, Conscious choice, Intention, Attention)

My essential question or wondering this week is:

_____

Find at least three memories of Collapsed Time; try to find both types: time slowing down and time speeding up. What is the connection between your thoughts and what is happening?

This Week's Practice
1. Place your attention this week on time—how fast it seems to move or how slow it moves. Become the observer of time this week. Does it seem to shift with your attention on it? Notice how time seems to speed up or slow down depending on your state of mind. Are you bored? Are you worried? Are you excited? Are you anticipating? Are you energized? As your states of mind shift, what happens to time?

2. Make a "to do" list for this week. Be sure to include everything you can think of that you would like to accomplish this week. You will practice following the energy within as it directs you to each task. Choose one to five activities on your list that are fairly important to you but do not have a scheduled time (appointment) in which to get done. As you gain experience in this, you can include all tasks, even those that have scheduled appointments or deadlines. For this week, choose up to five tasks (i.e. bill paying, grocery shopping, etc.). Creating a partnership with your essential guidance will mean listening for the subtle yet distinctive energy that prompts movement. Wait for the energy to move you to the particular task. Notice what happens to your thinking if you believe your task may not get completed. Do you get worried? How does it feel when you do the activity with energy and direction compared to doing it by the clock?

Extra

Choose one hour each day when you will follow the energy of your soul instead of the clock. Select different times of the day. Is it easier to do during certain times of day than other times? How might this affect your routines and sense of timing or the pulls you feel on your time?

For more, visit http://www.ILoveMyWhisper.com and click on "Audio Lessons Week 2."

Week 3: Urge

If you haven't read Chapter 4 on Urge, please return to that chapter and read it before doing these exercises.

The Distinct Experience

An Urge from your soul is the magnetic impulse and heightened energy and desire to move toward an action or outcome even though you do not always know why. You are drawn to give your attention to some action or some person.

The Essential Lesson

In the beginning, you may not sense Urges unless they are quite heightened. Urges can be very subtle, however, prompting a change of attention, so you may be sitting having a cup of tea when suddenly you feel nudged to put the clothes in the washer—not as a *should* but as a sudden desire to do so. Perhaps later, you notice that you needed the very shirt you washed and now it is ready for you.

Locating Urge

1. Do the Anchoring Meditation (Appendix A). For a guided meditation on audio go to http://www.ILoveMyWhisper.com

My essential question or wondering this week is:

_____

2. Find at least two times when you have been urged to do something and you followed the Urge. What happened? Write it in your journal. Be clear as to how Urge feels within you. Where do you feel it ... in what part of your body? Is it a flutter? A pull? Be as specific as you can. This is your way of receiving signals.

3. Find a time when you felt urged to do something and you didn't. Perhaps you were urged to call someone and you didn't, or perhaps you were urged to leave the office earlier and you didn't. What happened?

4. Can you find in these examples the distinctive feelings of Urge? What does your heart want you to know in those experiences?

This Week's Practice

To place your *attention* on the sensations that guide movement, ask, "What do I do next?" Wait until you are urged to take a particular action. You can recognize this from how it felt in the past, (#2 above). This may be very subtle and come as a thought: *Do the dishes; take a shower; get some milk.* You see, we sometimes think guidance is only about the big things in life and comes with a burning bush or lightning bolts. We are guided all throughout the day. This week, tune into the subtle urges you receive and try to do this at least once per day.

Notice how your mind wants to jump in and tell you what to do based on your "to do" list. Pick a time during the day when you have nothing in particular that needs to get done and ask, "What do I do next?"

Extra

What is procrastination? Well, we think of it as putting off or delaying doing something, right? If we follow the urges of our guidance, would everything we think we need to get done get done?

I finally learned how to clean my house. I used to set aside a particular time during the week and force myself to clean and do laundry. I hated it. Then I noticed if I did whatever was in front of me, whenever I was prompted to do it, the house not only got cleaned, it stayed clean. Now I clean a little at a time and only what I notice and am guided to clean. It works beautifully. Try it. Take the task you normally put off or procrastinate about and wait until you receive the loving thought to do it … and then do it. Do you notice more energy for the task?

Remember, you have access to audio lessons on our Web site that supplement each week's practice. Go to http://www.ILoveMyWhisper.com and click on "Audio Lesson Week 3."

Week 4: Wonderment

If you haven't read Chapter 5 on Wonderment, please return to that chapter and read it before doing these exercises

The Distinct Experience
Wonderment is the feeling of amazement and awe, especially when a question or wondering you had is answered in a surprising, often astounding, way. The two types of questions that give rise to wonderment are wondering and the essential question. You will practice both this week, noticing the surprising and delightful ways your questions are answered.

The Essential Lesson
Wonderment shifts the vibration of worry, doubt, fear, concern, and indecisiveness into amazement, joy, surprise, and delight. We are then able to magnetize our heart's desires from this place of higher vibration and alignment.

Locating Wonderment
Do the Anchoring Meditation (Appendix A) and select a specific way to tune into the soul's voice.

This week I will use _____to tune in.
(Noticing, Conscious choice, Intention, Attention)

My essential question or wondering this week is:

_____

Wonderment is one of the easiest experiences to locate in your life. You are so awed or surprised when it occurs that the event is memorable to you. What you may not remember readily is the question or wondering you asked, and so you may not have realized you were given a very direct and distinct answer. Find at least two times when you were amazed by something that occurred in your life; you were delighted and surprised by the event or circumstance. Write your story in your journal.

Can you locate the question you had asked that you wanted an answer to? Were you trying to decide about a job or perhaps wondering about taking an offer of some type? Perhaps you were considering a move to a different location or looking for specific information about something. How was the answer from Wonderment different than the one you would have given yourself?

This Week's Practice

This week, you will begin to notice the means your soul self uses to capture your attention. You may want to review Chapter 14, Interactions with Your Essential Whisper. You have particular ways to receive guidance, ways that are easiest for you and align with your intrinsic design. You may be more visual and see images, like dreams or symbols. You may be more auditory and hear sounds, like when LaRue heard her phone ringing, and be more receptive to verbal messages and songs. You may be more kinesthetic and sense or feel easily within your body and feel magnetic pulls or sensations in your gut.

This week, become aware of your Essential Whisper's primary channel of communication with you.

1. What is your heartfelt desire this week or your essential question? Write it here:

_____

2. This week, notice all the information you receive that answers your question. Keep a journal handy and nearby so you can jot down words or dreams as they occur.

3. Pay close attention to the qualities of Wonderment—surprise, delight, peace, joy—as you get your answers

4. Notice the difference in those qualities in #3 above and what happens when you attempt to give yourself an answer.

5. What stands out for you? What are your primary ways of receiving answers? You will use this information Weeks 7 and 8.

Extra

What are you worried or concerned about this week? Use this week's practice to turn your worries into wonders. Select one or two major worries you have. Rephrase these worry statements into wondering statements like you did in Chapter 5, in the Find Your Whisper Moments, page 42. If you did not complete that exercise when you read that chapter, go back and take a look; and if you have the desire to, do it this week. If you did complete that exercise, did you receive guidance about your wonder statement? Did you forget you had wondered? Are you still worried about what you originally put down? Remember, you are asking your inner guidance for help and directing wondering to that infinite source.

For audio supplements, visit http://www.ILoveMyWhisper.com and click on the week you would like to listen to. You may also download a *free* Whisper Practice Journal that corresponds to this eight-week program. Enjoy!

Week 5: Knowing

If you haven't read Chapter 6 on Knowing, please return to that chapter and read it **before** *doing these exercises*

The Distinct Experience
Knowing is the very distinct feeling of sureness about something, without knowing how or why you know it. It is a feeling that seems cellular and internal, not mental.

The Essential Lesson
Knowing is high recognition of something already known to you on the soul level. It is alignment of the highest order with your unique soul print, and it matches the desire for a specific experience, including illness and death, so that compassion, forgiveness, and love rise from those and become the ultimate experience. The more in alignment you are with your nature (soul), the more you experience Knowing and act surely and resolutely. Decisions are effortless in Knowing.

Locating Knowing
Do the Anchoring Meditation (Appendix A) and select a specific way to tune into the Whisper.

This week I will use _____to tune in.
(Noticing, Conscious choice, Intention, Attention)

My essential-question or wondering this week is:

_____

Remember a time when you knew that you knew. Later you shouted, "I knew it! I told you so!" What did you know? This isn't when you had a strong belief about something—this is when you had no clue how you knew or why you knew. Go into the feeling of Knowing and feel the sureness of it. Write your experience of Knowing.

Now find a time when you believed very strongly about something and you later found out you were wrong. You learned that what you believed turned out not to be true. Describe the differences between these feelings of strong belief and Knowing. Get comfortable with how each of these feels.

This Week's Practice

Strong beliefs can feel like Knowing and get in the way of being able to discern the difference. We all have strong beliefs about certain ideas, and this week you will practice making your beliefs a bit more flexible.

1. Each day, write down five beliefs you hold and feel very strongly about. Some of these may be about your children, parents, the world or community, money and work, and so forth. For examples of the hundreds of beliefs we may hold, go to http://www.ILoveMyWhisper. com and click on "Beliefs."

2. Say aloud one belief you wrote down. Feel how this belief is true for you, perhaps even resolute.

3. After you have stated the belief and felt how it feels within, now state, "But I could be wrong."

4. Notice the feelings that arise. Do you have any resistance? Do you think, "No way! I am not wrong about this!"

5. Find just one reason this belief might be wrong.

6. Notice the feelings again. Any shifts?

7. Repeat for the other four beliefs.

Here is an example:
Belief: If my daughter doesn't get good grades, she won't get into college.
Feeling: Notice how the belief feels. Calming? Stressful? This belief can be a bit scary if my daughter isn't getting good grades and I believe she needs to go to college and won't get in.
New statement: If my daughter doesn't get good grades, she won't get into college, *but* I might be wrong!

Notice your feelings.

One reason: There are thousands of colleges that use many assessments for admission. Or, lots of people have gone on to college who did not have high grades in high school.
Notice feelings: Actually that feels better, more peaceful …

This practice will help you to open your mind and notice how beliefs can be right and wrong, good and bad. You also will get really good at discerning strong beliefs from Knowing, and that is its real purpose. Beliefs have been with us for a while, and Knowing can appear quite suddenly. If it is really hard to admit a particular belief might be wrong, then go to the Resistance and Values Procedure in Appendix B and do the exercise detailed there. You may also find an audio supplement for this procedure at http://www. ILoveMyWhisper.com.

Remember this is *not* saying the belief is wrong or you are wrong for having it. This is just a way to crack the mind open a bit and open your heart to new ways of seeing your world.

At the end of the week, you will have reviewed and opened up to thirty-five beliefs! Congratulations! You are becoming flexible and open to hearing your Essential Whisper!

Extra
Listen to things you don't agree that others are saying and state, "You could be right!"

Week 6: Inspiration

If you haven't read Chapter 7 on Inspiration, please return to that chapter and read it **before** *doing these exercises.*

The Distinct Experience
Inspiration is the infusion of ideas, along with high energy to create that idea. Often, the idea doesn't seem to be directly related to your goals or plans, yet it fills you with a strong desire to act on what you are envisioning. When acted on, the connection of the creation to your regular routine becomes apparent.

The Essential Lesson
We are creators. We are inherently designed to create; it is natural and inborn within our soul. Many people say, "I am not creative," and so creative energy is discounted and not acted on. Denying your essence to create will cause many of the discomforts of resistance. There are many opportunities to create: courses, recipes, crafts, tree houses, costumes, writings, art, businesses, … the list is endless. When you are hit with a surge of inspiration, act on it; all that is needed is given you.

Locating Inspiration
Do the Anchoring Meditation (Appendix A) and select a specific way to tune into the Whisper's voice.

This week I will use _____to tune in.
(Noticing, Conscious choice, Intention, Attention)

My essential question or wondering this week is:

_____

Find a time when you were completely and utterly inspired to action. Can you find it? You couldn't wait to get started. You may have had doubts, but you acted on the inspiration anyway. Write out your story and include the idea that came to you. What did the energy feel like? Be specific. Locating these qualities shows you how you receive these sensations.

Now find a time when you were inspired to do something, but you didn't do it. Perhaps you were inspired to paint or draw, and you went out and got all the supplies, but you didn't paint or draw. Look around. What do you have unfinished that *originated* as an inspiration? What happened to the energy? How did it feel?

This Week's Practice

Have you noticed that all of these qualities are energy shifts with distinct feelings of higher, lighter, vibrant, and energized sensations? Inspiration comes with an intense shift of energy to create. It may be that what you create will inspire someone else or help someone to feel good, light, and positive.

1. Locate any beliefs you have that tell you that you are not creative or inspirational. Write those down, and follow the Resistance and Values Procedure in Appendix B and zap those beliefs!

2. Your *intention* this week is to create something you are inspired to create. Don't worry if you are not feeling particularly inspired at the moment. For now, simply state your intention.

3. Although the energy of Inspiration is sudden and intense, it is not always long-lasting. You may be inspired for a few minutes to write down a quote you just heard, along with your thoughts about it, and when you are done, the energy leaves. This week, begin to notice the short bursts of Inspiration you receive, and practice acting on every single one. You may be inspired to pick up the knitting you put down and work furiously on it for hours, and then the energy will leave. Simply notice how Inspiration works for you. What is important is to follow it, follow the energy of it.

4. If you still find it difficult to feel Inspiration then go to something that inspires you and fills you with deep joy and wonderment. Do you get inspired by certain music? How about literature? Does going to home improvement stores inspire you? What about nature, trees, animals? Whatever it is for you, these are your natural connections to inspiration. Immerse yourself at least once this week in something inspirational to you.

Extra

Keep a running list of all the ideas that come to you. As you receive an idea, write it down using colorful pens or use colorful Post-its® and stick them in your notebook. Jot them all down, even the crazy ones! This is a practice in not censoring, letting ideas have their life in you without any guilt about acting on them. If you are energized to do so, then by all means, get going. We tend to miss Inspiration because we lump all ideas into the same "can't do them now" bag. No idea has to be given any more life than the energy it takes to record it. When one flies in that captures your attention and comes with a burst of energy, then that's your baby. Your Whisper is saying go for it.

Weeks 7 and 8

Congratulations! You have completed the first part of the Practice Guide, locating all six of the Distinct Experiences. Now that you know how each of these experiences has played out in your life and you recognize the sensations of guidance, you can create and design your unique partnership with your Whisper.

During the next two weeks, you will give attention to your intrinsic values, which arise from the natural, inherent, individualized (not separate) essence of your being. You will notice the extrinsic values you hold and see how they are distorted. This conflict is what causes stress.

Also, during these next two weeks, you will become intimate with the way your Whisper interacts with you.

Week 7: Aligning Intrinsic Values

If you haven't read Chapter 12, Your Intrinsic Design, please return to that chapter and read it **before** *doing these exercises.*

Description of Intrinsic Values
The intrinsic design is your individualized life design or blueprint, which supports within you certain gifts, talents, values, experiences, and ways of being in this world.

The Essential Lesson
To really understand attracting our hearts desires, you must fully understand that our values are what receive our attention. We are attracted to our values: any person, place, or thing that promises to fulfill our values or anything that threatens to violate our values (or a previous violation of our values still unresolved). What you have in your life right now, what you do in your life right now, and what you see in your life right now shows you what you value. You have already attracted what your attention is on. To attract what you value intrinsically, place your attention on those values.

Locating Intrinsic and Extrinsic Values
Do the Anchoring Meditation (Appendix A).

If you haven't already completed the exercises in Chapter 12, Your Intrinsic Design, please go back now and complete them: Uncovering Your Intrinsic Values, and Uncovering Your Extrinsic Values.

Some of my intrinsic values   Some of my extrinsic values

_____   _____
_____   _____
_____   _____
_____   _____
_____   _____

To really see how values direct you attention, and to experience the pull they have in your life as you go about your daily activities, notice where your attention naturally goes. Continue to do this until you have a full experiential understanding of the impact values have on your life.

For example: *I used to have client appointments fairly early in the morning, and although I have always enjoyed these appointments, I disliked having to start my day so early. I really wanted to meditate and get a workout in, but I found it difficult to say no to requests for morning appointments. I thought I needed to see clients when they needed to schedule appointments, or they may choose not to come at all, thinking I was an unaccommodating facilitator. This was a* should *in my life; I should put my clients first before my own personal desires. My intrinsic value for personal health and well-being, however, was being ignored, until I simply became exhausted—which, as you know by now, is a symptom of resistance. I now honor my intrinsic values of personal wellness and freedom to create my day as I desire, and I continue to have a busy practice that begins somewhere around 11:00 AM, after a quiet, contemplative morning.*

Keep a journal of what you notice your attention is on throughout the day, including the predominant thoughts. This will tell you what you consider important.

This Week's Practice: Attracting Your Heart's Desires By Aligning Your Intrinsic Values

1. List something you would like to have (attract) into your life. Perhaps it is a dishwasher, a new job, a new car. Make it fairly small, yet specific, for this exercise. Once you get the hang of this, you can do this for anything.

Let's say you'd like a new car.

2. You will now take your *intrinsic values* and apply those to your desire. So let's say your intrinsic values are trust, decisiveness, and generosity. How do those values relate to the car? Perhaps you want a car you can trust, that is dependable, reliable. You want to be decisive in your selection—how much you will pay, when you intend to get this car. Perhaps you do not always give yourself the best and cut corners, so now you will be generous with yourself and get some of the options you would like, perhaps a sunroof or a newer make and model.

    Do you see how this works? When you align your intrinsic values with your desires, it gets very exciting; you become uplifted and energized and open to possibilities. Your desire is strengthened, and you feel empowered to take the next steps. You are in alignment.

3. Now that you know what you desire *and* you have matched it up with your intrinsic values, ask your guidance what to do next. Then listen and follow any urges or inspiration. If a memory pops in that is a Snapshot-Click, pay attention to it. You have completed six weeks of tuning in to the Whisper's way of communicating with you; trust that you know this now, and watch the magic happen.

Week 8

You made it! You are now ready to create your own distinct practice.

This week, you will put it all together and design your unique, individualized, essential *daily* practice and partnership with *you*. Just as you brush your teeth every day, you will come to this practice as an easy, effortless way to commune with God. Talking to God, the open perfect place of love we feel, within, is as easy as breathing. Are you breathing? Good! You can talk to God. And now you know how God talks back.

Remember, your Essential Whisper is clearly discernable in its quality of love and peace, and this is *always* the case.

You are not alone.
Join our Whisper Community!

There's lots of information for you and answers to reader's questions. Check out our Web site at http://www.YourEssentialWhisper.com.

Read the amazing stories of how others, just like you, have followed their Whisper. To share your story, please post it at http://www.ICanHearMyWhisper.com

My Practice

➢ Anchoring Meditation (or you may design your own meditation).

➢ My best channel to **tune in** is _____
(Intention, Attention, Noticing)

➢ I **decide** (choose) to _____my inner guidance today.
(Recognize, Follow, Trust)

➢ The way(s) my Whisper speaks to me most frequently is through the
Distinct Experience of _____
(Snapshot-Click, Collapsed Time and Space, Urge, Wonderment, Knowing, Inspiration)

➢ The **interactions** are most frequently through

_____
(Dreams, synchronicities, my writing/journal, dialogue, words/songs, symbols, nature)

➢ It is hardest for me to hear my Whisper when _____

Or alternate: Yesterday or last week it was hardest to hear my
Whisper when _____
(I have a decision to make, I am at work, my family is around, it is about money or
finances, it is about health, Other)

Because _____
(Explain why you think it is hard or difficult)

Locate all of the limiting beliefs around this issue that you can.

For example:

• Yesterday it was hardest to hear my Whisper when I was rushing to
work and feeling anxious.

• Because I was afraid I would be late for work.

The beliefs around this issue *afraid to be late for work* could be:

• I should be on time for work.
• I can't hear my inner voice when I am rushing.
• I need more time to get ready for work.
• My husband should be more helpful in the morning.

- The kids should be more helpful in the morning.
- I should go to bed earlier.
- I need to concentrate on driving, not listening to my inner voice.

➤ Do the Resistance and Values Procedure (Appendix B) on the beliefs you uncovered above or any that you uncover throughout the day.

➤ Ask an essential question or a wondering or state your heart's desire.

➤ Journal and act on the answers you receive.

EPILOGUE

The End of the Story

By La Rue

❧ Frieda ❧

To this day, I find it astounding the surprising ways the Whisper weaves its magic in and out of our lives. It's like a giant basket being woven by hands from above.

Off and on for weeks, I had a gnawing in the pit of my stomach. At first, it was subtle and I didn't really notice it. The feeling started off more unconscious and transparent than obvious. One early morning, two weeks into the gnawing episode, I was awakened by a startling dream. I lay in bed completely restless while thinking about my eighty-six year old mother, who the dream was about.

I turned on the light to see what time it was. 5:20 AM. *Should I call her? Is she okay? Has she fallen? Did she die in her sleep? What if I call her and she's dead? What if she has gotten up to go to the bathroom, fallen, and can't get to the phone? What if I call and I wake her up? What should I do? What would I feel worse about, calling and waking her or not calling and later discovering that she needed an ambulance?* I looked at the clock again; it was now 5:25 AM. I had just experienced five very long minutes of anxiety in the pit of my stomach.

I picked up the phone; it rang and rang and rang. No answer. I hung up and called back. It rang another twenty times. No answer. Maybe I'm dialing the wrong number. I called again. Another twenty rings later, no answer. *Okay, I must notify my sister since she can get to Mom faster than I can, I thought to myself.* I wrapped my bathrobe around my shoulders, walked downstairs to retrieve my sister's phone number, and the Whisper urged me to dial Mom one more time. She answered! Whew! Relief!

She told me she had been in a deep sleep and it had taken her a while to get to the phone because she doesn't have one in her bedroom anymore. "You mean you don't have a phone beside your bed? What if you need to call 911 in the middle of the night?"

I apologized for calling and waking her. She assured me it was okay and told me that she was glad I called so that I could put my mind to rest. Before she hung up, she asked about the dream that spurred me to call. I told her that she was sick in my dream. Being the direct and humorous lady that she is, she asked, "Was I sick, or was I dead?" We both laughed and said good-bye.

I went back to bed but couldn't go back to sleep. That gnawing feeling was still there, even though I knew she was okay. After a discussion with a friend a few hours later, I realized there was something I needed to say to my mother, and that the day would not end without me expressing it live and in person. I flew into action, rearranged my schedule, headed off to buy her a new set of phones, and hopped in my car for a little road trip to see my sweet mother.

During my visit, we spoke frankly and openly about death, just as we have for the last four years. She talked about the last time she saw her mother alive. I expressed my gratitude to her for allowing me to talk to her about the inevitable death of the body that's to come. I thanked her for not pretending that it isn't going to happen. She told me she knew it would be good for me to be able to talk about it with her while we could still exchange words.

Standing at the door, as I was saying good-bye, she kissed my lips three sweet times and hugged me over and over and over with her skinny little body—the whole ninety pounds of it. She then gently but firmly placed one frail little bony hand on each of my shoulders, looked deeply into my soul, and spoke the most tender words to my ears that I had ever heard from her—and I'd heard a few in the last four years. She told me why she chose to name me Freida.

"I knew a lady named Freida. She was the softest, sweetest person I had ever met. I liked her so much. She was so very kind, gentle, and tender. And that's what you've turned out to be. You're so sweet, so soft, and so kind. I see I chose the perfect name for you."

She had told me that before, but not with the love and tenderness that was being expressed that day. And, for the first time in my life, I actually received her communication. We did our final hug, and as I drove away, mother, as she always does, stood in the window, blowing me kisses until I was out of sight.

By the time I got back to Dallas, the feeling in my gut had almost completely dissolved. By morning, it had completely lifted, and I felt as light as a feather. A shift had occurred. It felt like my life force energy was flowing again and that all was well. The comfortable, familiar feeling that I have come to know oh so well had returned: the feeling of peace.

I'll never be able to explain the mystery that intimately connects us all to each other. Nor would I even want to. I love the mystery. One thing I do know for sure is that a completion needed to take place between me and my mother before she said her final good-bye. The discomfort paid a visit to awaken me to the reality that the completion needed to happen and it needed to happen now. Discomfort was my friend early that morning. It caused me to wonder, to inquire, and to explore until I got its message.

Today, after that intimate exchange between Mother and me, for the first time in my life, I don't silently cringe when someone calls me Freida. I smile. Sometimes, I cry tears of gratitude as I quietly celebrate the abundant love in my life and a name only love can give.

Appendix A

The Anchoring Meditation

The Anchoring Meditation anchors the mind and places the attention on your heart.

Read the following meditation once or twice, and then close your eyes as you practice its instructions. You may want to read it into a tape recorder and play it back while you sit or lie comfortably and listen to it.

Also you may listen to the audio of the Anchoring Meditation by going to http://www.ILoveMyWhisper.com.

As you sit or lay comfortably, begin to relax and focus on your breathing. Notice the cool air as it enter your nostrils and the warm air as it leaves. Pause.

As you are ready, allow your eyes to close, becoming aware of the muscles around your eyes and forehead. Pause.

Allow those muscles to relax completely. Completely relax, allowing the tension to flow away. Pause.

Bring your attention to the top of your head. Relax the top of your head; let it feel open and expansive. Allow the feeling of relaxation to flow down, down, all the way down to all of the muscles in the face. Completely relax. Pause.

Relax your mouth, the corners of your mouth, the jaw, the tongue. Relax and let the tension melt. Pause.

Now, bring that feeling of relaxation down your arms, relaxing your shoulders, all the way down to the tip of your fingers. Pause.

Bring that relaxation down into your torso and all the way down into your legs. Pause.

Now, bring the feeling of relaxation all the way down, right down to the tip of your toes. Pause.

Allow yourself to be totally, totally relaxed. Long pause.

Now, we are going on a journey to your inner sanctuary, the home of your sensations, the place in your body you feel open and unrestricted, expansive and unlimited. Imagine yourself in a most peaceful place; perhaps it is a forest, seashore, a mountain top, or right where you are. Notice the sounds in your place of peace. Pause.

Imagine the vibrancy of the colors and textures. Pause.

Take a deep breath in and smell the incredible aromas. Pause.

Feel how fully alive you feel in your place of peace. Pause.

Now, you will anchor this peace into your body by allowing a golden shaft of light to surround and infuse you. Pause.

Allow the light to settle in your body where it does. Notice where the light goes and allow it to travel. As it stills and lands, notice where this loving light settles. Anchor the light in place in your body.

Thank the light for anchoring itself in your being, and notice where this shaft of golden light anchors. Pause.

Stay here for as long as you like. Before you leave your sanctuary, place your attention on the anchored light and ask your Whisper what it wants you to know. Pause.

Thank your Whisper for its perfect guidance and begin to come back by feeling the sensations of your feet (small pause), your legs (small pause), your torso (small pause), and your fingers and arms (small pause). Allow your face to stay relaxed as you bring your attention to the muscles around your eyes.

When you are ready, in the next few moments allow your eyes to open as you bring your attention back into the room and your present surroundings.

Write down any impressions or messages you received.

When you want communication with your Whisper, simply become still and focus your attention on where the light anchored itself.

We invite you to share your stories of how your Whisper has spoken to you and continues to speak to you.

Share yourWhisper stories by visiting
http://www.ICanHearMyWhisper.com.

Appendix B

Resistance and Values Procedure

This procedure is deceptively simple yet astoundingly powerful. Use this any time you have a symptom of resistance or a belief or thought that causes you discomfort and/or blocks you from the awareness of your Whisper's distinct messages.

Breathe evenly and deeply as you do the following:

A. Identifying

1. Determine the belief or symptom of resistance that you would like to release.

_____

Example: Life is not fair.

2. On a scale of 0 to 10, with 0 being *none* and 10 being *highest*, what is the level of discomfort (stress) you feel when you think that belief?_____

   The goal is to get that level down to 0, so that you feel no stress when you hold that belief in mind.

3. Determine the intrinsic value you want to activate.

_____

Example: I am a fair person.

B. Releasing

4. While gently tapping the temple area on both sides of your head (between the outside corners of the eyes and the ears), state aloud the following statements twice while inserting your belief statement:

With love for myself, I release all beliefs that/about

_____

Example: With love for myself, I release all beliefs that life should be fair.

With love for myself, I release all perceptions that/about

_____

Example: With love for myself I release all perceptions that life is not fair.

With love for myself, I release all judgments that/about

_____

Example: With love for myself, I release all judgments that life is not fair.

With love for myself, I release the need to believe

_____

Example: With love for myself, I release the need to believe that life is not fair.

5. Now what is the level of discomfort (0–10) you feel when you hold that belief in mind? If higher than a level 2, repeat #4 above.

C. Activating

6. Imagine a huge clock in front of you where the 12 is on the ceiling and the 6 is on the floor directly below you. Keeping your head and chin level, you will move your eyes around the clock while stating aloud the following, inserting _your_ intrinsic value.

Eyes up at 12:00, breathe and say aloud: I am _____

Example: I am fair.

Eyes far right at 3:00, breathe and say aloud: I am _____

Eyes down at 6:00, breathe and say aloud: I am _____

Eyes far left at 9:00, breathe and say aloud: I am _____

Eyes back up to 12:00, breathe and say aloud: I am _____

Eyes center, straight ahead, breathe and say aloud: I am _____

D. Affirming

State the following while gently tapping you temple on both sides:

"I easily and effortlessly recognize, trust and follow my Essential Whisper. And so it is!"

You may do this procedure as often as you like.
To download copies of this worksheet, visit http://www.ILoveMyWhisper.com

These procedures are adapted from Evo-K™ and Emotional Freedom Technique® (EFT®).

A fabulous source of information is a Web site by Emotional Freedom Technique® founder Gary Craig, http://www.emofree.com

Appendix C

About

❖ Evolutionary Kinesiology™ ❖

(Evo-K)

The need, and seed, for Evolutionary Kinesiology was planted over twenty years ago as LaRue found she was face down, wallowing in a pool of failure and longing to leave this earth. When suicide looked like the one and only way to end the suffering, spirit intervened, showing her that her only option was to get well. A series of synchronistic events unfolded that lead her into learning the art and mastery of applied kinesiology—a gentle and effective way that immediately sliced through unconscious blocks, getting to the heart of what was *really* going on in her life and finally resolving it, once and for all.

Literally transformed by the experience, LaRue began to help others remove the blocks that were impeding their lives, success, and evolution. Word of mouth spread, and soon her schedule was overflowing with desperate people looking for a way to end their pain and suffering, to unlock their inner treasure, and to live fully. Desperate lives were quickly changing into happy ones, and soon people wanted to learn how to do what LaRue was doing. They wanted to pay it forward by helping others transform as they had.

After years of prodding by clients, friends, and acquaintances to share her knowledge and life-changing expertise with them, she acquiesced, and Evolutionary Kinesiology was born.

At first, LaRue thought she would teach one course only. She thought the people would be satisfied and would leave her alone. But that didn't happen. They wanted more! As people began to talk to friends and family scattered across the United States and abroad, classes grew from LaRue's living room and into living rooms and healing centers in various states, including New York City, and eventually even to England.

Since her first session almost nineteen years ago, and after thousands of clients and several thousand hours of life-changing sessions, Evo-K™ continues to evolve. LaRue and her Evo-K Facilitators continue to pass along this methodology to those who are drawn to it.

You can learn more about Evo-K and the levels of training at http://www.Evo-K.com.

Chapter Notes and Resources

Introduction

1. Evolutional Kinesiology™ (Evo-K), formally known as the SoulTalk Method, is a unique method of obtaining biofeedback from a person's own subconscious using Muscle Response Feedback, a most advanced method for making the unknown known and revealing your innate wisdom to realize your highest goals, dreams, and ambitions. To learn more about Evolutional Kinesiology, please visit http://www.Evo-K.com

2. Muscle Response Feedback, also known as precision muscle testing, is done by placing a very light touch to the client's outstretched arms. The arms will either hold strong when gentle pressure is applied or will weaken in response to words, images, or certain physical stress tests. It shows an accurate indication of the type and amount of emotional stress that the client is dealing with. In the sixties, Dr. George Goodheart discovered that the body could be used as a device to communicate with this wisdom directly. By testing a group of muscles while introducing sugar to the body, Dr. Goodheart found that tester muscles would either remain strong or would weaken. He called this technique applied kinesiology, which later became known as muscle testing. Through muscle testing, he found that the body will tell you which foods or substances are healthy and which ones are harmful. Harmful stimuli

will create stress and cause the body to weaken, while healthy foods will make the muscles test strong.

In the seventies, Dr. John Diamond further researched applied kinesiology in the scientific community. He validated the claims that the tested muscles would weaken in the presence of artificial sweetener and test strong in the presence of natural sweeteners.

Dr. Diamond's theory also showed that the body would test strong when the individual tested would think positive thoughts, feel positive emotions, or make a positive statement. Research also showed that negative thoughts, emotions, or statements would cause the tested muscles to weaken. This new research was to become known as behavioral kinesiology. You may find it interesting to know that smiles were found to make the body strong, while criticism caused the body to weaken.

Research continued into the nineties, when Dr. David Hawkins and Noble Prize winner, Linus Pauling, PhD. researched and documented theories, people, and works of art, and found that theories, persons, or works of art/science could be validated as to their truth and accuracy.

3. David R. Hawkins, MD, PhD was the first to recognize the correlation of muscle testing (kinesiology) as a biofeedback mechanism for determining the validity or truthfulness of something, which he delineated in his book *Truth vs. Falsehood, How to Tell the Difference*. In this seminal work, Dr. Hawkins describes in full detail what he calls Levels of Consciousness, a calibration scale on which all things known can be placed and from which the level of truth can be determined.

Prologue

1. A Course in Miracles, Published by the Foundation for Inner Peace, Mill Valley, CA, 1992

2. One Brain, a system developed by Gordon Stokes and Daniel Whiteside, co-founders of Three In One Concepts, teaches that specialized muscle testing obtains biofeedback using the proprioceptors in the muscles as they interact with the subconscious brain. Precision muscle testing uses both arms simultaneously, thereby accessing the right and left brain hemispheres as well as the front and back hemispheres. This allows direct contact with all levels of self-awareness. The introductory meeting for One Brain was at that time held in the

Dallas area. This system was still relatively new, and facilitators and trainers would travel to offer classes in various cities throughout the United States. It has since become international in scope.

Excerpted from "Improve Learning Awareness" by Gordon Stokes and Daniel Whiteside, Three In One Concepts, 2001, West Magnolia Boulevard, Burbank, CA, 1996, ISBN 0-918993-77-6

3. Dr. John F. Demartini is a leading inspirational speaker and author at the forefront of the personal and professional development industry. A chiropractor, his scope of knowledge and experience spans thirty-four years, and his extensive research and studies cover thousands of writings and hundreds of disciplines. Dr. Demartini is founder of the Breakthrough Experience—a revolutionary approach to personal transformation. To learn more about Dr. John F. Demartini, visit his Web site at http://www.drdemartini.com

Chapter 8

1. The Inner Advantage Training program is a six-week tele-seminar class and home-study course that leads students into a deeper understanding and practice of recognizing, trusting, and following inner guidance. To learn more about this course developed by Vanessa and La Rue, please visit, http://www.InnerAdvantageTraining.com

2. Hawkins, David R., MD, PhD. *Truth vs. Falsehood*, Chapter 7, The Physiology of Truth; Axial Publishing, 2005.

Chapter 9

1. *Merriam-Webster's Collegiate Dictionary, Deluxe Edition*, 1998 by Merriam-Webster, Incorporated.

Chapter 10

1. *ReSurfacing: Techniques for Exploring Consciousness, Exercise 6,* Harry Palmer, Published by Star's Edge International, Altamonte Springs, Florida, 1994 .

Chapter 11

1. Hawkins, David R., *Truth vs. Falsehood*, pgs. 76–77.

2. Byron Katie experienced what she describes as "waking up to reality" in 1986 and since then has introduced a process she calls The Work to hundreds of thousands of people throughout the world. The Work is a process of inquiry using four questions, which has enabled hundreds of thousands to investigate stressful thoughts. To learn more about Katie and The Work, visit http://www.thework.com.

3. For more information on how to contact a qualified Evo-K facilitator, please visit www.Evo-K.com.

Chapter 12

1. *The Divine Matrix,* Gregg Braden, Published by Hay House, Inc., Carlsbad, CA, 2007.

Chapter 13

1. *The Secret*, Rhonda Byrne, Beyond Words Publishing, Hillsboro, OR, 2006.
The Secret, DVD video, TS Production, LLC 2006.

2. *The Law of Attraction, The Basics of the Teachings of Abraham,* Esther and Jerry and Hicks, Hay House, Inc., 2006.

Note: The testimonials and stories highlighted throughout the book are from real people. Their bios and contact information may be found at www.YourEssentialWhisper.com.

RECOMMENDED READING

There are many outstanding resources to read and explore for further information on the processes and concepts referred to in *Your Essential Whisper*. This is not an exhaustive list and is given only to get the reader started on individual research and exploration. Your *Essential Whisper* is written from the direct experiences and inner guidance of its authors, and listing these books does not imply material was taken from or extracted from these resources unless noted within the body of this work.

Power vs. Force: The Hidden Determinants of Human Behavior, by David R. Hawkins MD, PhD, published by Hay House, Inc., is the seminal work researching the reaction of muscle responses (the positive of a hold or the negative of a release) to various stimuli and has correlated this with the human organism's ability to discern truth from falsity.

Loving What Is by Byron Katie, published by Harmony Books, 2002, introduces the revolutionary inquiry process called the Work and offers several real life examples that depict that the root cause of suffering begins with the identification with our thoughts. It offers four simple questions that cut to the truth and dispel illusion.

I Need Your Love—Is That True? written by Byron Katie with Michael Katz and published by Harmony Books in 2005, continues where her introductory book leaves off and explores in depth the inquiry process applied to the beliefs related to seeking love and approval outside ourselves.

The Promise of Energy Psychology: Revolutionary Tools for Dramatic Personal Change by David Feinstein, Donna Eden, and Gary Craig, published by Penguin Group, 2005, is an easy-to-understand guide to energy and meridian tapping techniques alongside energy balancing processes.

Workshops and Classes

- **Join us for our Free Tele-seminars**

  www.WhisperTeleseminars.com.

- **Would you like a deeper experience of Your Essential Whisper?**

The Inner Advantage Training 6-week Tele-course helps you to recognize, trust and follow inner guidance with absolute certainty. You receive over 24 hours of guided, interactive instruction and coaching. Listen to an audio message by visiting

  www.InnerAdvantageTraining.com.

- **Receive your complimentary weekly on-line publication.**

The Weekly Whisper arrives by email each week. Each issue has a feature audio recording that gives you useable and practical tips to help you live your life joyfully as you effortlessly trust and follow your Whisper. Subscribe now at

  www.TheWeeklyWhisper.com

- **Stay up to date on all the class offerings, ideas, and helpful information.**

  www.YourEssentialWhisper.com

- **Find out about the special programs offered by La Rue.**

  www.Evo-K.com

- **Find out about the special programs offered by Vanessa.**

  www.BodyvoiceTechnologies.com

A special thanks to our technical partner, Carol Cody,
who began with us when this was all just a vision.
www.carolcodyweb.com

Journal Page

Journal Page

Journal Page

Journal Page

Printed in the United States
132095LV00001B/21/P